CU00658386

How to Lead for Daring New Leaders

The No-Nonsense Guide to Develop Basic
Leadership Skills. Discover Your Power to Be
in Charge

Paul A. Wyatt

© Copyright 2022 - All rights reserved.

The content contained within this book may not be reproduced, duplicated or transmitted without direct written permission from the author or the publisher.

Under no circumstances will any blame or legal responsibility be held against the publisher, or author, for any damages, reparation, or monetary loss due to the information contained within this book, either directly or indirectly.

Legal Notice:

This book is copyright protected. It is only for personal use. You cannot amend, distribute, sell, use, quote or paraphrase any part, or the content within this book, without the consent of the author or publisher.

Disclaimer Notice:

Please note the information contained within this document is for educational and entertainment purposes only. All effort has been executed to present accurate, up to date, reliable, complete information. No warranties of any kind are declared or implied. Readers acknowledge that the author is not engaged in the rendering of legal, financial, medical or professional advice. The content within this book has been derived from various sources. Please consult a licensed professional before attempting any techniques outlined in this book.

By reading this document, the reader agrees that under no circumstances is the author responsible for any losses, direct or indirect, that are incurred as a result of the use of the information contained within this document, including, but not limited to, errors, omissions, or inaccuracies.

Table of Contents

Introduction

The pessimist complains about the wind. The optimist expects it to change. The leader adjusts the sails.

—John C. Maxwell

We embrace our knowledge of leadership according to the people we follow and those who stand out from the crowd.

We can say leadership over the last 120,000 years of existence on this planet shows that our species developed and evolved because we formed tribes and elevated stronger members to guide and hold the community together. This is no modern practice.

But as the centuries passed, we came to understand the role in the new world and how we could evolve the practices of leadership to better fit the picture. More concepts popped up, more theories emerged, and more and more people began playing with the social science of being a leader and guiding countless followers in a certain direction. Now everyone wanted to manage, control, and have a more impactful influence.

Information written by strong, independent, forward-thinking people who truly thought their method of leadership was the one to adopt led many to success and many to failure. Leadership was now a title, a position, a spotlight for fame and fortune, and no longer the pure concept it was meant to originally be. This troublesome consistency in the 21st century is where, sadly, the incorrect information and demoralization in the choice of being a leader has bred a mentality and perception that hinders human connection and team spirit many times over.

It is increasingly difficult to look for the right answers. Simplifying the most courageous ideas of leadership did not always mean that individuals with completely different perceptions on life, careers, and their personal relationships would address that gap and make it an opportunity to grow together.

The challenge all aspiring leaders face today is choice. The amount of information that is out there about this subject is mind-boggling. An internet search can bring up over 700 million results that leave a person feeling overwhelmed and uneasy.

It is rather scary to see that over the years all these models and their various concepts have meshed into a vast and perplexing conglomerate of, essentially, personal perspectives. It is natural for the brain to feel stressed about the sheer amount of information out there that could or could not be beneficial to your character.

The principle of choice basically states that the fewer options we have, the better we are able to make a clear-cut decision. A restaurant menu with only 10 choices is going to be a lot less stressful to the brain than one with 50. We would prefer to have fewer choices with higher values so that we can subconsciously move forward and not feel like we have missed out on something better. Fewer subdivisions and more answers to leadership and life, in general, could be considered the solution, allowing it to be easier to find what you are really looking for and what those around you deserve.

The world needs better leaders, it's a fact. We need people who want to occupy a station of service to their fellow humans besides them. The question is, how do you find your way into leadership? Or, how do we discover the spark within us that allows us to be the leaders we envision for ourselves?

The truth here is that leadership is actually rather simple. I am not saying it is easy, by any means, but in its basic steps and requirements, it's simple. But finding your own way to calculate the end result on your own shoulders is the tough part. Reading a piece of literature that gives you the principles and shows you the way is marvelous, you understand the point and the mission statement of the whole idea. Although, when you close that book and attempt to put it into practice it is a different story altogether, right? We start sweating and pondering on the actions and reactions of each choice because maybe we do not fully comprehend what the book was asking of us. The overachieving, overthinking, overworking mind will doubt itself and make mistakes of judgment. And that, my dear reader, is precisely where the lesson lies, in the knock-on effect of learning.

There are some crucial points about destructive or uninformed leadership that need to be put forward and consulted. That of self-interest, aggressive behavior, and negative environmental influences. You can almost feel sorry for people who you can see do not belong in the role of leader. Not because they are simply bad at it, but because they have not been shown the right way. They might be living within a world that does not justify the needs of others and that is something you cannot crucify them for. Their past lessons learned were superficial, their understanding of dealing with people is superficial, and they only see the superficial side of the choice.

My name is Paul Wyatt and thanks to my two-decade career of counseling, coaching, and educating countless future leaders and the organizations that surround them, I am able to bring to you this complete and thoughtful book that gives you an idea of where and when you should be making those paces forward to achieve personal and corporate success.

The fact that you have picked up this book and made a single choice out of the hundreds of others is brave to begin with and smart overall. This book will give you all the principles and primary motifs that you could ever need to begin your journey into the big world of people. Because that's essentially what leadership is, a business of people and making it your business to know yourself and them better each and every day.

Initially, we will explore the meaning of leadership and the basic styles that surround it, defining the roles and characteristics of each. I will be showing you the developmental skills required to master your vision, and then we touch on the why and how of finding self-awareness in your role. By understanding the essentials—communication, interpersonal strategies, and the concepts of making the best decisions by using critical thinking and mental models—you will be able to see the picture with better clarity. Finally, we address what it means to be a leader in the 21st century after crashing through a pandemic and a terrible year of doubt.

I would like you to understand this one thing very clearly: We all have the quality of leadership, and all it needs is a reason to shine. With anything in life, before you make that choice, you need to know your "why." Why do you want to lead? And why should anyone want to be led by you?

Depending on where you are in life and what environments you have created around yourself, it establishes a certain character, a certain philosophy of self, and a solid reason! All leaders have something fundamental in common: they believe in something with all their being.

Do you think this is where we begin to peel off the outdated leadership layers of workforces and communities alike? When will the new, shiny, and beautifully flawed leaders come to show the world that so much more is possible when you do it with thoughtfulness and purpose?

It is easier to be unhappy, moody, greedy, aggressive, short with people, and exclusive. It is so easy to take things with impatience and haste, steering away from meaningful connections with others and steering towards personal connections with financial gain and image. What is far more complex and ultimately rewarding is showing love, empathy, patience, and being guided by a sound moral compass. That is the solution to destructive leadership in its entirety, finding that doing the hard things tests our human nature and capacity to care about something bigger than ourselves.

The leader this world needs is not a leader that wants the easy way up. The world needs a hard leader that is willing to do the hard work of building others to great heights with everything they believe in.

Dearest reader, because this is a beginner's guide, what I suggest you do is keep a pen and paper close at all times. It is highly advised that you assess what is written in each chapter and make your own observations of the character you believe yourself to be now, and who you could be in the future. By applying some new methods to the pursuit of honing leadership skills and being a kinder, more empathetic individual, new doors will surely open. It would be beneficial for you to become more connected to your core aspects that bring you closer to self-awareness and knowing that leadership is learnership.

Now that we are ready to jump into the meat of this holistic book, I hope you enjoy every minute of it. I feel confident in knowing that, even though you are unique and have a broad and diverse worldview from others around you, that this piece of writing will open your eyes to a dimension of guiding others so they may guide you in turn.

1

Introduction to Leadership

A leader is one who knows the way, goes the way, and shows the way.

—John C. Maxwell

D ue to the gravely vague assumptions of leadership over the last two centuries, not many can honestly describe what leadership means and what it stands for in its purest form. Most answers revolve around business acumen or the ability to take charge of difficult situations. This is because personal perceptions and past experiences mold leadership to be something that it was not intended to be.

There are so many different scenarios that require a leader. Teams in sport, teams in business, and teams in the family all need strong leadership. Starting with parents, to employers, to teachers, to military commanders, politicians, sports captains, coaches, and intellectuals in their respective fields. These are positions of potential leadership, where great people come to thrive and some, unfortunately, fall short.

You are most likely questioning all the qualities and motifs for ever wanting to be a leader in the first place. It must be a whole lot easier to follow than it is to lead, right? Wrong! They both fill a strong purpose in life. Without one, there cannot be the other, and if one or both parties are weak in will, knowledge, and respect, then the whole system collapses in on itself.

The world is changing in such a way that the more knowledge the newer generations have about evolved leadership the more it contradicts those of older generations that are currently sitting in top positions around major corporations. We are slowly beginning to see that millennials entering the workforce are more disenchanted with superiority and influential control that they will find it hard to keep a job. They are (almost unconsciously) fighting the system, by rather passively showing uninterest and zero concern for the rank and theme that has been established over time and wanting leadership that brings depth and shows real concern for the people and their environments.

We notice that many potential leaders begin their journey with the best intentions. They are motivated, keen to make impactful decisions, and prove themselves. These new leaders have gone through the formal training, gotten their tertiary qualifications, and are now ready to jump into a rank that they believe they deserve.

These new leaders might understand what technical skills are required, but have they adjusted their mental capacity to involve others in their new journey? Unfortunately, we see more and more people using this as a stepping stone, not a foundation. They will show how they care, how they stand up for and make decisions that revolve around people, and then later when things get complicated and cold, they will forget and abandon those markers of interest for bigger and brighter opportunities to influence and mark smaller, more niche groups of people, that will enhance their role and wallet.

So, let me enlighten you on the purest concepts of leadership and what core motifs are behind the term.

What Is Leadership?

Leadership is so often over-defined that it can be a rough ride seeing where your own characteristics fit in. Over the last 30 years, more than 850 definitions of this skill have filled the work world and confused people on whether they have what it takes to step up and make a difference in this ubiquitous field. It sounds odd when we talk about the concept as a whole because, at its core, it is a beautifully simplistic thing.

Too often, we hear the phrase "natural born leaders" in media and corporate settings. I like to think that this initial baseline is unreasonable for one main reason: more leaders are nurtured into their role than born into it. The true leader knows that leadership was a choice they made and a choice to be a role model by seizing their opportunity in this tough and sometimes cruel world.

In its most simple form, leadership means you have followers. You are surrounding yourself with effectors that react to your stimuli. You have sights on a future world that could exist and you are showing those followers that you could never do it alone. Because that is not the nature of progress.

We can say that leadership is a process, a never fully stable or fixed methodology and it evolves according to the people around it and the place in which it is needed. It can be thought of as a practical skill or a research setting where more intricate facets of the profession are analyzed.

Leadership at its core is a service! Yes! In fact, a good leader knows that they are serving a higher need. A need for direction, purpose, and the beauty of the collective coming together to make something out of their time and energy. When the followers really respect and enjoy the challenges that the leader has put forward for them then input and communication are entwined in the growth of the group as a whole.

Know that leadership is not about the rank, the position in which you sit, or the amount of money that you make each month. Leadership is not about pining for the spotlight and power control that comes from directing a group of individuals. You are not leading those behind you, you are leading those next to you, those who are not very different from you and who seek greatness on their own terms.

If you have one person, just one, who believes in you and respects your guidance and decisions, then you are a leader! You are leading a belief and helping others towards a better world with higher moral etiquette. You find true satisfaction when you see that the followers are in love with the path you have created for them, or better, the path that you have shown them and one that they can create in their own individualistic manner. By allowing them to see the benefits of your choice for themselves, you are immediately upping your game. Your actions are not forced and hovered over, but passively (and in a clever manner, which we will delve in a tad later) actioned with intent, conviction, and trustworthiness.

Do yourself a favor and jot down all your previous experiences with employers, coaches, teachers, and family members who have judged themselves as leaders in an environment. I would like you to assess what impact they have had on your life in terms of experience, knowledge, and lessons learned. Rank them in your own way, depending on how you have perceived their value to your life. Maybe you know someone who also shared this experience with you, so take initiative and ask them what their perception was of that person in a leadership sense.

The best way to understand leadership is to understand what it is not. If your list consists of people who brought you positive reinforcement, understanding, diligence, and respect, then you most likely have a very good concept of the skill. But if you have a list of people who never saw you as a person, who never involved you in their bigger plans for the future, and saw you as just a number, then you will make sure to never be that type of leader to your future followers.

You are embarking on a lifelong journey to greatness, remember that. Once you have decided to be this truth seeker and truth speaker, then you will always be called to this choice. Even if later in life you end up distancing yourself from leadership, it will come back to you one way or another, asking you to hold a responsibility that you know, deep down, you could never reject. Once a leader, always a leader.

The Qualities and Characteristics of a Leader

Now that I have described what leadership is in all its forms and functions, I would like to take you through the various qualities and traits a leader should possess when they begin their voyage. These characteristics should not be forgotten or overlooked when a leader is distracted or consumed by the wrong influences that sometimes plague a "position of power." Rather they should be cherished and held close like a burning flame in the dark. It is vital that a person remembers the true values whenever they find doubt in their actions or in the environmental influences around them.

Qualitative leaders:

- **Are proactive**
  They solve the problem before they react to the mistake. It is so easy to jump up and down and make a scene about what went pear-shaped. It is far harder to sit back, ask how you can help, and involve the right people to get the mess cleaned up and move forward. Remember, we are not here to do the easy, but the hard! The repercussions of someone's mistake are not forgotten but pushed aside until the time is right and everyone has calmed down.

- **Do what they expect from others**
  By putting as much responsibility (or even more) on their own shoulders as they do on their followers, a leader shows strength in accountability and forward-thinking. Every so often, a manager will hide behind their position or sweep an error under the rug, instead of showing the team that they can also be vulnerable and human. Nothing brings people together more than the presence of

a leader who understands what it is like to fail and what it means to get right back up and try again.

- **Create positive energy around them**
Team morale is conducive to productivity, and the leader knows that better than anyone. They know when it is time to grind and when it is time to play. Both productivity and comfort in an environment breed incredible amounts of positivity. I do not state that a leader needs to be the extroverted person that arrives at the office on a Monday morning jumping off the walls. What I would like for you to understand here is that positive energy can be active and passive, equally powerful in its own ways. Sometimes the passive method works even better, as it calms the team down and still gets them amped up to enjoy their day and enjoy their job. Subtle motivation, a strong physical presence, and wearing a smile more than a frown will create such an environment.

- **Delegate with more care**
A leader will learn (through trial and error) how to manage other people's time in accordance with their own schedule. By allowing more complex tasks to fall on their own shoulders and giving more time-consuming and generalized tasks to others, it can both quicken the process and give a sense of responsibility and achievement to the team members involved. A leader will begin to read between the lines and know who in their team has the correct skillset for the specific task, while at the same time involving those who stay below the radar and giving them an opportunity to shine and pick up new skills.

- **Are decisive**
  Having confidence in a decision is what builds a leader's credibility and trust in their team. They stick to their choice and bring a sense of stability and core value to their persona and style. When a leader knows how to make small decisions with dexterity and a no-fuss attitude, they have developed a strategy model that keeps these small decisions flowing into bigger solutions. While those big decisions are made with care and consideration, they know the power of talking to others and asking for advice when needed, and when to sit back and make that decision on their own.

- **Become more approachable**
  I say this because any human being needs time to adjust to their team, and being approachable on the first week can almost feel fraudulent when a leader is just all out there and open for advice. But true approachability means that they have gotten to know who is around them better and can read scenarios involving different individuals with a humble and empathetic eye. This approachability is physical (open-door policy, smiles, eye contact, and interactive mannerisms) as well as emotional (a storyteller, humorous, overall personality). The leader's job of allowing for others to have comments, input, and feelings about tasks throughout the project or time-space is imperative.

- **Communicate with intent**
  Words can be weapons to destroy a relationship or elevate it to new heights. When a leader learns how they use their verbal and non-verbal language around others, they automatically move

up on the leadership ladder. There is a fine line between being a nice person and a tough boss. The trick comes into play on the when and where to use the correct method of communication. Situational differences, personal differences, and environmental influences control how the message is relayed and received. The great leader uses eloquence, subtlety, directiveness, empathy, and wisdom to do their job and to allow those around them to do theirs in the most enthusiastic and motivated way.

- **Are emotionally intelligent (EI)**
  This means that they have the capabilities to perceive, reason, understand, and manage their emotions. This same principle is applied to the emotions others feel around the leader and how that leader resonates with them. A certain amount of wisdom is required to build EI and previous experiences in family, work, and love create a filter that resonates with others. A good leader always attempts to acknowledge the cognitive dissidence (conflicting beliefs) in themselves and in others, and find a self-awareness that shows courage and transparency.

These qualities are a baseline of what any leader should hold. Good and great leaders evolve and dissect these qualities further (which we will touch on later) so they may learn more along their journey. Mastering self-control while always having an open heart is something that takes time.

Now, what about the characteristics and traits a leader should possess? The six traits below assemble what the leader needs to advance or bring along with them onto their journey of personal and career success.

1. **Problem Solving Skills**. These revolve around problem deconstruction, generating solutions, and a sense of self-regulation.
2. **Social Capacities**. These traits align well in emotional and social intelligence, as well as an ability to negotiate and persuade.
3. **Motives and Values**. Here, we see a motivation for leading and bringing about socialized empowerment. The traits often involve a value of achieving on a regular basis.
4. **Expertise and Knowledge**. This encompasses traits belonging to the knowledge and experience one has in their respective fields.
5. **Cognitive Capacities**. These traits touch on the general ability to use creativity, intellectual adaptability, and the complexity of cognitive power.
6. **Dispositional Attributes**. What we see here are the personal attributes of being open, extroverted, flexible, and most of all understanding risk.

Therefore, what we understand here is that arriving at the start point of your journey already equipped (or in the process of equipping) with these qualities brings you a better chance of success through every experience.

Be sure to come back to this chapter when re-evaluating what it means to be a leader. As I mentioned, the more you can return to the principle motifs, the more you learn to incorporate them naturally into your path.

Roles of a Leader

The definition of a leader often describes a role without a position. I have given you various concepts to mull over, and these are perceived according to what environment you are situated in. To use these roles in every type of leadership you maintain is the secret to success. So let me give you the five distinct roles any potential leader should begin to fill:

1. **The Mentor**

   Leaders are first and foremost aware of their influence. Most importantly, they need to be aware of their primary purpose to build and develop more leaders around them. The need to use empathy and care for others so they can do the same for their peers is the magical ingredient. This role evolves along with the leader's experience within their field of interest and within their team.

2. **The Motivator**

   This is where the leader sees through the veil that people sometimes wear at work. Grasping what each person is truly motivated by is like using a fine-tuned tool. Some destructive leaders use this role maliciously, veering followers into paths that only hurt them. But when it is used ethically, the leader can evaluate with precision what they want, appreciate, and aspire to, and use that to elevate the whole team together. When the leader can also recognize achievements in his flock, then he knows precisely how to reward them.

3. **The Learner**

   As I have stated before, I will state again: leadership is learnership. That is a fact and a rule. It is callow to think that the skill required will passively pass into our understanding, like osmosis. What it really requires is a person to be a lover of learning and be keenly aware of the blinders that are limiting their view. Always interested in knowing more about their surroundings and their work. Improving their methods and their overall understanding of their sphere so as to increase human and organizational potential.

4. **The Navigator**
   Many leaders understand this role quite well, and at times it, unfortunately, becomes the focal point, leaving the other roles to gather dust. The leader has sights on a goal and this goal will be accomplished before the set time required. When time management and human resources are combined efficiently, the leader can really begin to put forward tasks that make a difference and that challenge the team's capabilities. There should generally be zero ambiguity in handling situations, where the leader's peers (other team leaders) are working in optimal conjunction with one another. Teamwork, as well as team coordination, is vital.

5. **The Communicator**
   The use of proper language through cohesive thought is something I will be mentioning many more times in this book. When a leader understands this role well, then many of the above roles will fall into place around it quite nicely. A good leader articulates with care and always requires some kind of feedback on what was said. Questions are a leader's best friend along with an even tone of voice and an open demeanor. Always attempt to

improve the way you naturally express yourself so as to have more control over what is said and done.

When assessing your own capacity to lead through these five roles, consider carefully how each can be broken down even further, according to your current situation or worldview. These blueprints of leadership need to always be reflected upon with caution and fairness. If you fall short in one space, it is not the end of the world because the learning bit is the fun bit! Always be ready to take up some attributes by pursuing your curiosity and your sheer will to grow.

Defining True Leadership

It is safe to say that now you must have a much better idea of what leadership entails in its primal form and function. So, let me give you what I believe to be (over many of the years studying this phenomenon) true leadership.

It is accepted that we give so much of ourselves to our children as our parents gave to us in our childhood and that true parenthood had no return value on the 'model'. Being a good parent is purely about taking your time to see the value you added to their lives and what they make of it in their own capacities. Parents do not sit there with their outstretched hands palm up, waiting for you to pay back all the money and emotional stress you placed on them all those years. The reward was seeing their child be better, brighter, and bolder than before, shaping a path that was inspired by their value.

The same thing applies to true leadership, but what can be overly defined and never truly exemplified is not a justifiable action.

Therefore, "something that typifies you as a leader, the expectation of people following you is this; that you will develop them as leaders. So, no matter what your credentials say, you become a leader only when you are able to develop future leaders" (Walia, 2020). Focusing more on the input rather than the output is a critical part of the curriculum of growing as a better person amongst your followers.

True leadership sows the seeds of innovation, perseverance, and commitment so that the whole team may reap the rewards of success and personal development.

There is no power struggle, no lack in guiding with expert knowledge, no shame in making mistakes, no misguided information. The only thing a true leader has is the strength to get back up when times are tough. Fight battles that might not mean winning the war but getting everyone there one step at a time.

The tragedy comes in when someone of rank, (not a leader, please remember the difference) thinks, "What do I get out of helping others to achieve greatness?" or, "Why should I be expending energy on teaching and instructing others to lead themselves when they might just challenge my position?" What will they lose? Will it be financial, or for the worse sake, prideful? That is a terribly, terribly sad emotional turmoil that comes from always expecting something in return. You want to avoid this imbalance at all costs!

The role of a leader is definitely not to sit down and calculate what time, patience, and understanding is spent on the people and what profits or values get returned. To live a life that gives back, returns two-fold, rejoices in seeing others around them grow taller and stand on their own two feet, that's incredibly special!

You deserve just as much as those you guide. Sure, the perks are cool, but remember that you are in the same league, you are in the same recognition. Your position gets you nice gifts, but you deserve the same as your weakest link and your weakest link stays close to your wing.

Do not stand on the pedestal with your hand on your hips waiting for people to blow hot air into your direction. Get off and sit next to them so they can feel your humanity and humbleness. The greatest leaders were not standing at the top of the windy mountain pointing fingers at those below. They were right there, on the cliff face with all the others, pushing and empowering them forward. Advancing in the world means being warriors together!

A true leader knows when to ask for help, so who guides the leader? People are at their best when they find someone who believes in them, therefore true leadership means also looking up to someone who has ticked a few more boxes than you. You are not above it all and if you stop pretending to have everything under control at all times, others will run in to help. Learn to take care of them and let them take care of you by relying on each other.

Remember, we spoke about communication? Well, surprise, surprise! Here we are at it again. Communicating as a true leader means waiting for everyone else to have spoken and then have an opinion. The skill to keep your opinions to yourself until the last moment will better your judgment of the conversation overall. As the great Nelson Mandela once said: "Practice to be the last who speaks."

2

Made to Lead: Leadership Self-Awareness

Wisdom tends to grow in proportion to one's awareness of one's ignorance.

—Anthony de Mello

A knowledge base on multiple fields of interest characterizes great leaders as something of polymaths in their respective spheres. The more a leader can learn privately within themselves, and within their other intellectual interests, the more impact they can have on their followers. Philosophy, finance, law, international culture, science, psychology, arts, and many more usually show up in the Wikipedia files of the greatest leaders.

Apart from the obvious, more illustrious choices in careers and backgrounds, the primary focus these great leaders implemented was on themselves. On their own perceptions, realities, and emotion control. The more they collected and stored, the more their world revealed its true colors.

Finding your true purpose and being more sensitive to the emotions bubbling within requires a substantial amount of self-work. I mean this by evaluating carefully what goes on within our egos and how we can stop negative thinking before it takes hold.

Two very prominent research analysts in the mid-90s did a study on the community of management and business in the US and stated clearly, "If the study revealed any universal truths in leadership development today, it is that the process should be transparent. Only by sharing the 'rules of the game' can an organization unleash the leadership potential of its employees." (Williams & Cothrel, 1997).

When a leader reflects carefully on what their influence means to others, then a curtain shifts away and reveals the answer of transparency. By not holding back and shying away from reaching out to those who follow you, and openly inviting them to watch and listen to what you do, how you do it, and why you do it, then you are becoming! Your knowledge is not a golden egg of possession but a goldmine of information and passion transferal that could be shared with the world.

These self-evaluations of character should be something that occurs throughout your leadership. Perhaps you should be asking a more powerful question: how trustworthy am I? Do I believe in my own words? Do I stand by them with pride?

The answers come from one place, and one place only: your pattern of self-assessment. Remember when I said that a leader's best friends are questions? So, ask yourself questions all the time. Keep yourself looking within so that you can purify your mental state and work with others in a clear and uncluttered way.

How Leaders Are Made

The skill we call leadership is vast and never-ending. A circle of growth and change, where information and adaptation permeate the core values of the term and bring forth leaders that have courage, flexibility, and empathy with those around them.

It would be extensively disingenuous if we assumed all leaders were born into it. The majority were made by utter perseverance and the constant priming of more fitting values that align with their characters. The fundamental flaws of our humanity are precisely why we are always discovering and charting new ways forward. That is our canon, our story. Therefore, it should be equally valuable for us to start charting new mental pathways and new ways of seeing the world around us.

Leadership manuals began to find fame when ultra-wealthy CEOs started writing, "I do this, I wear this, I write this, and I say this. If you want to make money, do what I do." The misconception of what really makes a leader and how they can reach for their dreams was worrisome, to say the least. That is where things started taking a turn for the worse and a negative mental shift appeared. The true message of leadership got buried like a forgotten artifact and overlapped by newer and grander ideologies of power.

Sure, there are always better ways to do something, as long as that leader is not stepping over anyone along the way. Tony Robbins, the American philosopher and coach, famously said that the strongest force in the universe is a human being living consistently with his identity.

So, by being true to who you are, and the chatter within your head, then you can learn how to focus on it or turn it down. There are four great ways to get more in touch with yourself:

1. **Keep a journal**

   People interested in staying close to their subconscious keep journals. When you start enjoying writing out your thoughts, worries, stresses, and joys throughout the day, you can learn to resonate with them better and study yourself with more interest. The improvement is tremendous for mental health, and the more you are interested in yourself, the less concerned you are with all the smaller negative events that might occur during the day. Write well, write honestly, write from the heart.

2. **Create a vision board**

   Again, anyone who is interested in getting their lives into a structure and finding a focal point for their energy and passion uses their creativity to engage it. To better envision a plan for the future, you would retrieve images that represent your wants and needs and stick them together to bring about a total collaboration of short, medium, and long-term goals for yourself. Or you could create a digital board on your computer or laptop. There are tons of free apps out there that can help you source images and motivational phrases to create something digitally unique as well as accessible in work settings.

3. **Focus on wellness**
   The body is a vessel that takes you to where your mind points. If your mind is always running but your body cannot seem to keep up, then it is time to put your health first. I am talking about drinking three liters of water a day, knocking back at least eight hours of sleep a night, doing physical exercise at least four times a week, and eating green, clean, and lean most days. These pointers will energize you and bring awareness to your surroundings.

4. **Seek the truth**
   The feedback loop is one of the only ways a person can get a better understanding of what others think. Yes, self-awareness is about your own perceptions being analyzed, but the subconscious cannot dig that deep! It requires an exterior analysis to fully complete the process. Asking friends, family, and colleagues about your characteristics of leadership (and those you lack) will heighten your pursuit of true leadership.

The investigative reporter David Epstein in his book *Range* speaks wonderfully about the concepts of self-awareness by expanding on match-quality. This points towards being more aware of your previous work, and previous employers you had, looking back at your careers, and using them as a diagnostic tool of your personality for better matches in future careers.

By pulling out your CV, you can start analyzing yourself a little bit more by assessing why you chose that job ten years ago, where it shone and where it stank, and seeing what influences it had on the person you are today.

Assessing past experiences in workplace and leadership settings is a fantastic way to open higher match-quality responsibilities as you progress in your career. If you fight your core aspects for a seat at a table where you will never have the ability to connect with people on a meaningful level and you solely interact with others remotely, then your core values as that leader will be suppressed and locked away in a dark room. Rather, find your natural inclination towards certain niches and make them work for you.

"The American Psychological Association published a study that found that given the dynamic and complex social environments in which most leaders operate, effectiveness requires them to possess certain perceptive and adaptive capabilities. Thus, these qualities don't just appear and they certainly don't develop in a vacuum" (National Society of Leadership and Success, 2017). That plainly states that nothing simply appears out of thin air. We are not magically transformed like in a fairytale, it takes time, the correct stimulation, and a certain positive mindset to become highly perceptive.

Therefore, we can say that leaders are made the same way as diamonds are made deep within the earth's crust. You need to let time, pressure, and heat transform you into something strong, beautiful, and clear.

Leadership Strengths and Weaknesses

There are two sides to the leadership coin: winning and learning. You either succeed, or you figure out how to not lose ever again. The strengths of a leader determine so much about their success, but what many don't understand is that their weaknesses do just as much, maybe even more.

If a person can be honest with themselves and deconstruct their persona into two columns of strong versus weak characteristics, then it can become a little easier to judge where you are flourishing and where you need more water.

You understand how the leader becomes a leader, but do you understand that a leader needs to resonate with both their accomplishments and their downfalls?

Please pull out that pen and paper and let us tackle what it means to take control of your narrative by looking deeper within using the strengths, weaknesses, opportunities, and threats (SWOT) technique. You begin listing your strengths and weaknesses by:

1. **Getting real with yourself**
   This means getting to know what your own ego displays to others for your own safety and what your ego displays only to you in those intimate and scary moments of self-awareness. This is something you would have done at least once in your life where disaster struck or luck prevailed. You would sit back, take a deep breath and suss out your honest reasons.

2. **Asking yourself the right questions**
   What are the strengths that have gotten you this far and what weaknesses have sabotaged you? Write a comprehensive list of these traits and what opportunities each has brought to your life. Are your strengths in keeping the ball rolling and

always having new ideas? Are your weaknesses in not knowing how to implement these ideas into action? Do your weaknesses allow other members of your team to shine? Find out what impact your traits have on those around you, too.

3. **What really makes you excited**
   If you think about it, what gets you revved up for a task or situation? These key aspects of knowing what makes you so eager to do something are very important to the process. You need to recognize your trigger settings of excitement versus nervousness. When something seems to be scary, maybe you are simply excited!

What is rather simple to do on paper is quite a bit more complex to perform in reality. The transition of what we preconceive something to be like and what really happens sometimes leaves people frustrated and confused. The thing is, this doesn't happen overnight. It is practiced slowly, carefully, and with a lot of self-love. By accepting who you are and who you are not, you are performing an act that, in itself, is already a major win.

Here are some of the powerhouse strengths that our emerging leaders would find benefit in adopting:

- The constant resonance with accountability and adaptability
- Having an eye and solid commitment to quality
- An ability to involve others in multiple situations
- Incorporating into communication plenty of thoughtfulness and reasoning

Far more glaringly intrusive to a person's character are their weaknesses. But by taking strides in understanding yourself better as a human being, then the weaknesses you see will become your leverage to better opportunities later, with greater chances to learn and evolve. Some shortfalls are:

- The lack of experience to be able to focus on the correct things at the correct time
- Not being able to express clear goals and tactics for the future with the team
- Lack of emotional intelligence and maturity that encourages understanding and patience
- A face-value comparison with peers by looking for approval and acceptance constantly on marginal and superficial aspects of the position held
- Problematic gaps appear between work life and personal life

By focusing on your strengths and encouraging yourself to always be searching within for more answers and motifs, then a core value as a leader will emerge. Find your main hold on a mentor or someone who sees value in you, where these people can guide you into calmer and more thoughtful choices. Their feedback is beneficial because knowing where your actions sit with others makes you re-evaluate and re-mold yourself. This is crucial in knowing how to better manage those stress levels by bringing along more pause and reflection with each situation.

Your Core Values as a Leader

The values you have had throughout your entire life, from the values your parents instilled into you to the values you collected from loved ones and friends, will be your platform on which you will be able to bring more and more people along with you into the journey of success and empowerment. The larger that platform, the more people can join you.

Expand those values and allow them to be the baseline of your leadership. Values can be overly generalized, but it is crucial that one understands that these values can lie in everyone in smaller and larger degrees. It is about harnessing these stepping stones and making them solid enough for more leaders to emerge.

- **Courage**
  A leader is someone who takes up that sword and fights for the values they hold dear. They fight for the people who hold those same values and they build a tribe that is willing to join their leader in the fight, too.

- **Respect**
  Everyone deserves to be respected firstly, as human beings, secondly, as a part of the team, and thirdly as an individual thinker and mover.

- **Modesty**
  You don't want to hear people talking about the car you drive, the brands you sport, or the office you occupy. You want to hear them talk about the business, their interests, their excitement in projects. Your image sometimes can attract attention that could be put to better use.

- **Service**

  It is first and foremost about your duty. Consider your service to those who follow you like the service a soldier has to their country. Yes, I know it's slightly outlandish when explained that way, but the concept is there. You are doing it for something you really believe in, something bigger than you.

- **Authenticity**

  Truth is one thing, authenticity is another. Be proud of the person you are! Let your light shine through and allow for people to see a side of you that can soften barriers and break the ice.

- **Integrity**

  Morals and principles are fundamental. These bring about integrity that the leader uses as their leverage. They are the unmovable force that keeps the team rumbling and rolling to new heights without breaking. It is like authenticity, but it requires a stronger emotional attachment to values.

- **Making a difference**

  The leaders we need are those that create new molds without creating more complex systems. Having interesting ideas means always looking for new information and expanding your radar. Making a difference means seeing what is missing in a group or environment and finding a way to resolve it with creativity and collaboration.

- **Wisdom**

  Learning to be emotionally intelligent and mature takes time. Great leaders have understood more of what they don't know and are willing to expand that knowledge without rushing. Knowing when to say something and when not to is wisdom. Stepping back and re-evaluating your preconceptions is wisdom. Caring more and taking less is wisdom.

These core values are either there, or are on their way. You can build them up by always assessing what characteristics you hold and what you probably should let go of (or tone down).

It is advised that you write down these strengths, weaknesses, and values and incorporate them into the models of leadership development that we will be addressing later. They will be the cornerstone to your growth.

3

Discover Your Leadership Style

Do not follow where the path may lead. Go instead where there is no path and leave a trail.

—Ralph Waldo Emerson

Now that we have discussed what leadership is and the values and qualities you should be focusing on, I would like you to start thinking about the next step of the process. And that is to find what style of leadership suits you, and where you can improve and remove certain traits so as to better your chances of being the best leader you can be.

In this chapter, we will plunge into the specifics of finding one that fits your character (if you haven't already) and assess further how you can evaluate or reevaluate your own.

There are so many different names, categories, and descriptions of leadership styles out there, it can really get tough trying to assess which suits your personality best and how your personality can converge with the requirements of each.

But it is crucial that a leader establishes a style that they can use to structure their daily tasks, emotions, and interpersonal relationships with the team. The fact is that leadership cries out for structure. Some people get away with just entering the ring unprepared and playing it by ear, but that sounds very stressful and often requires making more mistakes than are necessary. If a person already starts envisioning what kind of leader they want to be from the word go, then the path they graze upon will be a lot more straightforward.

What Is a Leadership Style and Why Is It Critical to Develop One?

In the late 1930s, a team of psychologists and researchers led by Kurt Lewin set their sights on developing basic categories of leadership styles present in a group of people. They began their research in schools where children would be evaluated by their reactions to situations and proposed stimuli. Three distinct styles came to light. First, an autocratic leadership, dictated by a command and control model of order to action. Second, a Laissez-Faire model, which demonstrated a lack of control, responsibility, freedom, and constant need for guidance. Third, the well-received Democratic style, which proved to entice people to want to achieve by allowing for votes of confidence and the groups' participation in decision and action.

Many more styles have been adapted and mingled over the following years. As the market for large corporations to build and grow in the early 20th century evolved, so did the idea of taking charge and becoming your own boss. In turn, this intrinsically grew more leadership styles as a larger group of diverse people entered the workforce and other top leadership positions. The market required self-evaluation and, as we see today, it is a widely popular topic in business and social science fields.

It is imperative that you understand each of these styles and consider all of them as a guide for when and how to use them.

"A leadership style refers to a leader's methods and behaviors when directing, motivating, and managing others. A person's leadership style also determines how they strategize and implement plans while accounting for the expectations of stakeholders and the wellbeing of their team" (Becker, 2020).

Defining a leadership style allows you to keep track of yourself and be fully aware of when to use it. What we understand now is that leadership is first and foremost about the self and the clarity with which the person speaks to others and how they speak to themselves. The boundaries of individuals are broken and bonds are formed in their place when values are adhered to. When leadership becomes more structured around the people, then fewer errors occur both in judgment and in performance. Remember, managing people is one thing, leading them is something else entirely.

The trick here is when and how to use these styles. Look, if you stay attached to one style all the way through your day, the rigidity of your leadership can disconnect from people around you. It is like playing a card game where you have all your different styles in one hand. You can choose to use a certain style depending on your situation and you can make an error when one style is used incorrectly causing conflict or confusion with peers and followers. If you can master a few different styles that can be interchanged and adapted according to the scenarios the leader encounters, then we can say that an understanding has been made.

Basic Leadership Styles

Below are some of the four most common leadership styles we see today. As I explained, there are various names for these styles in other sources, and sometimes the aspects of the style change, so I encourage you to assess the ones I have carefully brought forward for you to minimize confusion. Remember, the more concrete the concept is, the easier it is to make a choice and adapt it to your life.

Transactional

This leadership style is intentioned towards guidelines, rules, parameters, and standards of performance. It is probably one of the more common styles to implement and where a strong focus on the core bottom-line needs of the business comes first. A chain of command is established by the constant exchange system by which the leader gives tasks and rewards or punishes depending on the outcome. This automatically assumes that performance and behavior are aligned and set in stone.

Due to its subtle rigidity, this leadership style can suffocate long-term relationships and innovation within the company, but the efficiency and fairness (integrity) of this leader cannot be disputed when decisions need to be made and individual value appreciated.

This style requires:

- Structure and rules that allow the leader to avoid misunderstandings and mistakes within the team. For example, a solid contract that stipulates all the "yes" and "no" policies of the company, or large posters around the workplace that remind the employees of dress code and professional etiquette.
- Profuse communication about what they expect, what they stand for, and what (to them) the organization as a whole represents. This armor removes misunderstanding. Although communication might not necessarily be conducive to relationship building, it does ensure that the leader has addressed a concern, and the team has understood it.
- Creating a just reward and punishment system. Set rewards for set accomplishments need to be adhered to and respected. Sometimes a thank you is required, and sometimes a promotion. Sometimes a questionable look of disappointment, and sometimes a termination.
- Consistent monitoring prevents small mistakes from taking effect. The leader can choose to micro-manage in an active manner or react to an exception by taking a passive route. These should be used carefully and with the honest need to complete the goal, not show dominance.

The importance of defining the clear-cut punishment strategies should always be assessed early in the leader's choice of style and the theme the organization wishes to portray. This style can work in various scenarios, as long as the leader allows for some movement and input as well.

Servant

This form of leadership is solely focused on what the leader can do for the followers. This service model is extremely well accepted in more common situations with regards to followers being in doubt. The Servant provides assistance, encouragement, and resources along the way while putting their own career interests second. The power to give others power is where this model truly shines.

Due to the need to build strong relationships with followers, this style requires time to implement properly. The leader has a genuine interest in giving back completely to their followers, and that is why this leadership style is so rare. Trust in relinquishing power and serving as a real role model to others is consuming and can remove a degree of authority.

This style requires:

- Approval from the organization on whether this style can be implemented. It is a rather forward-thinking and altruistic method, therefore it might not be accepted if strong and steady leadership is required consistently.
- Advocate a very well-balanced mental state. This leader has looked within themself and recognized what they really need to do. A servant style needs to be honest and deeply embedded within the leader.
- The kindness this style brings with it is uncompromised. Building strong relationships and essentially becoming good friends with your team members means mentoring them into your role, entrusting

them with larger tasks, and packing loads of humility and forgiveness. Importance in maintaining these relationships is key.

This style can become a "walkover me" style if used too often, and should be selected in specific scenarios regarding emotions, honesty, and kindness. Many followers do not respond well to being left to their own devices and prefer a more action-paced leader.

By working around the aspects of high-impact leadership consisting of time, caring, and respect, you begin to treat the followers like you would treat your family members.

Laissez-Faire

In a nutshell, you have left the directions on the table, all neat and concise, and then stepped away to see what comes out of the followers' understanding of your instructions. This method of leadership gives plenty of freedom, and if applied in the correct setting, it can bring creativity and empowerment.

Although, when it comes to feedback and interaction between the two parties, this is left to a minimum, causing long-term detriment to the success of the organization. There is less motivation and direction and that in turn causes higher stress levels in teams with less experience.

This style requires:

- Having a team that knows exactly what to do. They are competent and know what is expected of them without needing supervision and support.

- Not needing to reward or punish followers as the leader keeps a distance from the operation in action.
- Trust and cooperation between followers become crucial. Here you would see one of the followers taking up their own mantle of leadership amongst their peers to help steer them in the right direction.

What we can understand here is that this style is very niche. The larger portion of companies and organizations in different fields would probably not prefer this method, and it would be advised that it be used in small strategic amounts. For instance, you could use this in challenger tasks so you may evaluate what level your team is running at. It is important that the leader develops methods for assessing their followers and knows what they are capable of.

Transformational

This type of leader is a storyteller. They are communicators by nature, and they open doors to self-evaluation and how each individual can make a difference. They are intellectually stimulating, supportive, and ooze inspirational confidence. The challenge they represent requires followers to want to improve their skills continuously and contribute to the organization in a creative and forward-thinking manner.

The leader could get very drained from using this style of leadership all the time, and it is more intrinsic to extroverted personalities who truly love being a part of many facets.

This style requires:

- Having a strong vision already implemented within yourself and your team. This leader knows how to entice and persuade their followers to achieve something that can change the organization or even the world.
- Tasks needing to run parallel with the vision set before the followers. Too much emphasis on the future can remove the effectiveness of the procedures that occur on a daily basis. Long-term success means balancing motivation and action.
- Commitment to executing the promises that were set before them. It is necessary that this leader always has the eye on the ball and does not under-deliver on their promise.

This leadership really performs well when a large change is due. When new energy and blood can bring a fresh perspective and more encouragement for optimal results, then it is successful.

I say again, these methods all work wonderfully when they are implemented in all sorts of environments independently. That is where great leaders are selected from the rest.

Leadership Styles Assessment Based on Action Logics

"Most developmental psychologists agree that what differentiates leaders is not so much their philosophy of leadership, their personality, or their style of management. Rather, it's their internal 'action logic'—how they interpret their surroundings and react when their power or safety is challenged" (Rooke & Torber, 2015).

The above statement was sourced from a study of different action logics done by Harvard Business associates back in 2015 titled, *Seven Transformations of Leadership*. They studied the answers of a certain group of leaders that would be placed into categories according to the results of the study. The percentages show how common or rare characteristics of certain action logics truly are and what impact they have on a leadership style.

Leadership styles are heavily based on what action logic the leader naturally possesses, therefore we can say that there are seven different types to assess which I have listed below. Have a look at the sentences that describe each action logic and choose the statements you agree upon and see where you fit more comfortably in each style.

1. **The Alchemist**

   Here, we see real social and structural change in society and the individuals within it. The Alchemist has the incredible ability to deal with many situations that pop up simultaneously at different levels. They constitute the 1% of leaders in the study, making them a rare gem indeed. When a person can generate all-around transformation by implementing physical, spiritual, and societal change, then we see leaders that make a mark on history forever! Hugely charismatic and holding very high moral standards for themselves, they create change by being the change.

   - A1. "A good leader holds empathy and moral awareness that helps their followers reach high potential."

- A2. "Whatever the task, there has to be a positive and profound impact made."
- A3. "My short-term and long-term needs are balanced well."

2. **The Strategist**

   These leaders constitute 4% of the study and we see these characteristics shining at an organizational and personal level. An intimate attention to leadership allows them to be highly aware of the world around them and find a keen interest in acquiring information and using it iteratively. They are very effective as a transformational leader and see the value of short and long-term changes. Holding a vigilant watch for opportunities and threats the Strategist is adept in transforming businesses and groups of people alike.

   - S1. "A good leader always strives for agreement amongst groups."
   - S2. "The individual achievement and growth of my followers are equal to the growth of the organization."
   - S3. "I can manage the stress and conflict in the team as I understand that it is inevitable."

3. **The Individualist**

   These types of leaders excel in communicating with all the other different types of action logic and constitute 10% of the study group. The Individualist has a skill for finding gaps in the system and resolving them with a performance strategy that is fluid. Their unique and practical mindset contributes tremendously to an organization as they are able to interweave their own approaches with that of others.

- I1. "Personal intuition always overrules the process of an organization."
- I2. "Being able to communicate complex ideas to followers requires relatability."
- I3. "Sustained success is nice, but progress is better."

4. **The Achiever**

   This category of action logic leans towards the managerial role, where the leader orient themselves more to the action and goal function. The Achiever stays close to market-related demands, but they also do very well when implementing more positive environments and systems around them to get the team delivering results. They constitute 30% of the group, making them the second most common action logic. At times, they show a downfall that stops them from seeing further than their four walls, but they tend to usually meet all their strategic goals set before them and balance people and their requirements with natural ease.

   - A4. "Managing the team is secondary to managing the market and bottom-line."
   - A5. "I understand how environmental happiness is expressed in production success."
   - A6. "Achieving success means following orders correctly."

5. **The Expert**

   Here, we see the most common action logic type amongst the group, constituting 38%. The Expert runs the show by using logic, rationality, and expertise in the product or system to elevate their credibility. Their rational efficiency guides them to be brilliant individual contributors to the organization but, unfortunately, rather poor inter-personal values. They might find it hard to relate to their team's needs in the long-term as they look for balance in numbers, statistics, and hard facts rather than social and environmental positivity. Emotional intelligence is not always appreciated, and their time could be better spent on their own work than in communicating with others.

- E1. "Pursuit of knowledge and expertise comes before the team and organization."
- E2. "My decision is usually the correct one."

6. **The Diplomat**

What stands out the most in this category is the notion that conflict should be avoided at all costs so as to bring people together and form group norms. The Diplomat constitutes 12% of the study and they will show great value in their collaborative characteristics. They have an innate way to bring people together. Unfortunately, their diplomatic ideologies rarely make room for improvement and innovation. Because of their constant need to gain control of their own behavior and appease the hig-her-rank peers in the organization, their followers would ultimately negate value from their positions.

- D1. "Instability appears when there is a change in the team."
- D2. "The social glue of the team removes conflict and resistance."
- D3. "Supportive roles and team-oriented activi-ties are where I shine."

7. **The Opportunist**

This group of leaders is found to be the most destructive in terms of social change and real leadership value. The Opportunist constitutes 5% of the study group and they are known to be great in emergency situations and at increasing sales strategies in the company. But they do not go any further due to their self-orientated ideologies and 'win no matter what' mindset. This can bring a perception of egocentrism, manipulation of individuals and their emotions, and a heavy sense of mistrust. Unless they evolve their leadership style and emotional intelligence, these types of managers do not stay in control for long.

- O1. "I am constantly in competition with everyone around me, even if that compromises my development."
- O2. "Rejecting opinions and observations from those around me is fine."

Now let's see where each answer reflected in the leadership styles:

1. Transactional: S1, S2, O1, O2, E1, E2, A3, A4, A6, D1, D3.
2. Servant: S3, A5.
3. Laissez-faire: D2, D3, E1.
4. Transformational: I1, I2, I3, A1, A2.

What I would like you to comprehend above all else is that leadership styles need not be set in stone. They need to be creatively and inclusively fluid. You can learn to adapt characteristics of one style and incorporate them into another if you wish, as long as your role as a leader evolves to complement these characteristics.

How Leaders Evolve

Evolution is inevitable. There has to be a space where previous observations get examined and new thoughts are put forward. There are some wonderful pieces of literature that bring to light the values of the evolved leader.

An American professor at the University of Houston, Brené Brown, wrote a book titled *Dare to Lead*. Here, she really breaks down what it means to be the brave, curious, and empathetic leader the world is looking for. She describes how characteristics of being vulnerable do not equal those of being weak and how they can evolve a leader for the better. Brown writes (2018):

> One of the most important findings of my career is that daring leadership is a collection of four skill sets that are 100 percent teachable, observable, and measurable. It's learning and unlearning that require brave work, tough conversions, and showing up with your whole heart. Easy? No. Because choosing courage over comfort is not always our default. Worth it? Always. We want to be brave with our lives and our work. It's why we're here. (p. 134)

So, we can comprehend that what this all boils down to is that a leadership style that is flexible and inclusive is optimal. By being acutely aware of who you are, what you stand for, and staying close to the same awareness of your followers, then you can lead with an authentic purpose.

When you ask yourself, "Why are they still following me?", you can assess some of your own answers from there, like: they have to, you deliver your promises, you help them, you are a friendly person, etc. The answers you get can help you stay on top of the meaning behind your leadership styles and the environment you create.

Another interesting book titled *Great to Good*, sees Jim Collins drive the development of the Hedgehog Concept into the world. This pertains to the business model and business strategy that a company can implement in order to excel in lesser diversity, but much greater knowledge and skill. In his book Jim writes (2001):

> Are you a hedgehog or a fox? In his famous essay, *The Hedgehog and the Fox*, Isaiah Berlin divided the world into hedgehogs and foxes, based upon an ancient Greek parable: "The fox knows many things, but the hedgehog knows one big thing." (p. 116).

This means making good decisions consistently, one after another, and accumulating specific knowledge over a period of time. Removing bravado and showmanship for others, to become a person who desires to understand the scene more accurately by asking more questions.

This method could easily be attuned instead to a self-evaluation of the leadership styles used to grow and evolve as a leader. Indeed, the world has now been developing leaders that hunger to know it all, do it all, and have all the answers. The fox is emotionally young but eager and energetic. They can be wonderful to be around, but heavily overwhelming and scattered.

The hedgehog is methodical and precise. More attuned to what is going on around them, their circle of followers, and their needs. Decisions are delegated correctly,

and focus is put on bettering the way the leader understands their community, business, and people. These two
characters are sometimes just different versions of the
same person with 30 years difference in age. Meaning
one thing: time was spent on this person. Lots and lots
of time. This hedgehog takes their time to learn some
things with exceptional focus, while the fox, in a sense,
has too many fingers in too many pies.

How much time is spent refining your strengths, while
on the other hand elevating weaknesses to higher levels
of awareness? And how much time is focused on people
and developing their individual strengths and weaknesses along the way? Alas, that is where the balance plays an
integral role and the leader evolves.

4

Proven Ways to Develop Leadership

In matters of style, swim with the current; in matters of principle, stand like a rock.

—Thomas Jefferson

We have discussed the leadership styles a person develops in synchronicity with one another as to better manage situations, emotions, and production. So, we can say that essentially, leadership styles are not static and the environment in which you use those skills dictates the style.

Now, let me jump right into the developmental side of things. How do we put into practice all the steps required to receive the golden chalice of service? Well, the evolution of the leader happens once they have developed into a person the followers admire and they themselves have pride in their actions.

Advancing in all the facets of leadership is important. We know that most of our previous employers had some kind of degree, diploma, or certificate to show that they had training, and experienced the general modalities in their field of knowledge. Yes, it is important, but it is more important to also broaden those fields and find better ways to learn and get that experience under your belt.

I would like to bring to your attention some of the situations you will want to insert yourself into so that you may become more aware of your developmental stages. I have also brought to you the models to base off of and what methods of learning you can grasp to receive the best stepping stones possible for the future.

The Three Variables That Successfully Develop Leadership

If you understand that leadership is equal to learnership, then we are on the same page. It is always striving to develop characteristics that shine through you and affect others in a positive and productive way. The effectiveness of a person's leadership is dependable on various aspects of personal traits and dispositions already present. Therefore, if one focuses on applying effort to maintain and build new skills in a constant and iterative way, that leader will see it as a gift that just keeps on giving.

It is said that "leaders new to their roles or who never received proper training can inadvertently and unintentionally drift away from their purpose and create a boss-watching culture" (Clarinval, 2021). What we can do to avoid that is by indeed always remembering the true purpose, which is to create a future-watching culture.

There are three main variables that influence how you develop as a successful leader:

1. When you are given <u>the opportunity to practice</u> skills that you know will improve your persona, position, and overall knowledge, then "no" is usually not the answer. Having the opportunity to walk through all the doors that open to you, devouring as much information and tricks of the trade as you possibly can, will create paths to new and exciting avenues. I like to call this the "sponge mode" where a lot of information enters, but a lot of the bad habits are squeezed out thanks to meaningful feedback.

2. Accepting that you <u>never stop learning</u>. Here, you will have to increase your own individual interest in learning new facets of the job. Your ability, and most importantly, your willingness is what will push you to learn and get very good at it.

3. Ensure that your <u>development program has struc-</u><u>ture</u> and critical content that honestly and clearly nurtures your true values and what kind of values you want your followers to see. It all starts with (you guessed it) a pen and paper, and the structure of a defined and clear program. You must build yourself a model and apply the method so that the improvement is step-by-step cognitive learning.

You will learn to get feedback on all situations tactfully. You will sign up for all the training that you can devour. You will have that mentor! And you will always take the time to reflect on what you did and what you will do. Keep both eyes on the now because the future is what you make of today.

Keep an eye out for online classes and ask around who might have more information on certain courses. Being proactive and asking your superiors what you could improve on and then making a budget sheet for the expenses is brilliantly bold. Showing interest in something really makes it hard for people to deny you the chance to learn.

Understanding Leadership Development Models

What does it mean to you when I say that leadership needs to be developed within the parameters of its function? Sounds a tad complicated, but think about it carefully. All kinds of leadership require a certain type of development. If you are a lead scientist running a lab with five assistants, your leadership development will be quite different from that of a flight commander running the team for a test flight.

"The leader-development process is rooted in a particular context, which includes elements such as age, culture, economic conditions, gender, organizational purpose and mission, and business strategy" (Lumen, 2010). In other words, having a leadership context impacts many of the development models.

Understating the models of leadership is like placing yourself at the architectural table and planning the design of a building. Your main job is to account for all the variables that come into play when drawing the plan on paper. The development is about putting your set intentions into that design so that others may occupy and learn from that given space for themselves.

For example, if your variables are set in the transactional style, then your boundaries would be rigid and the view limited, whereas in the transformational style, the view is three-dimensional and creative. The leader has incorporated their own values within the mental picture of development and understands how to use them.

Keep in mind that you are not the sole person within this developmental structure, account for the individuals that occupy it as well. And from those followers' influence within the design (when given the chance) change and positive adjustment can be made for the next leaders to stand up and, in turn, become the designers themselves.

Being open to many variables while still upholding a strong vision is the flexibility I am always mentioning the great leader possesses. You need to truly believe what is possible for them to believe what is possible. You are opening their eyes to a transparent and more inclusive world by allowing them to live within that design and influence it in their own way. Parameters and boundaries are kept until trust in others can allow for shared design with followers.

There is no best and least appropriate model to use. These models will depend on your own personal plans in life, your context if you will. It will change, hopefully for the better each time, but it would be pointless to hold on to outdated designs. Like many of the other leadership skills in this book, the developmental plan is evolving as the leader learns more about themselves and others.

Dear reader, take the time to always reevaluate who you are, who you look up to, where you have been, and where you are now. These cutting topics are the baseline for development and if you understand them, then you can incorporate honest and cooperative communication and the values of interpersonal growth.

Leading Leadership Development Methods to Try

There are multiple mechanisms that you could and should bring to your attention when expanding your knowledge in the leadership sphere. What you will notice is that these approaches to developing your leadership can be accessed independently but should be used in combination. The effectiveness of systematically increasing your own boundaries of expertise and insight, in turn, grows your love and appreciation for being a leader your followers need.

Here are some of the main methods used to get more traction on the road to successful leadership:

- **Formal training**
  A concern that you will find with training programs is the eventual inability to transfer what was learned in the coursework into practical work environments. As I explained before, reading something and actioning it correctly can be rather complex, even if what was understood seems so simple. This more traditional style of developing your skill set with study, examination, and feedback develops a good base, but it requires additional methods to really make an impact.

- **Developmental job assignments**
  The skills acquired after completing the training will need a place to go. Therefore, certain developmental tasks will be created and assigned to the future leader so they may learn, grow, and better understand their role and responsibility in the organization. This step is vital as it is one of the most effective methods of leadership development.

When a person can see, feel, and question all the stimuli of their role, their understanding of leadership increases even further.

- **360-degree feedback**
  I am sure you are now familiar with the importance of exterior input when leading others. A leader cannot stand alone and expect growth to always come from within. The enormous value of receiving full circle feedback from superiors, peers, and subordinates reflects the leader's ability to take that criticism, see where they fall short, and work on it. Or take that praise, tick the box, and ride it out. This person needs to be receptive and honest, making sure to accumulate as much data as they can from as many people as are willing. The larger the group, the easier it is to see the commonalities in their comments and build on strengths or break down bad habits from there.

- **Coaching**
  In this situation, a person has found a more mature leader to mentor and guide them to the next level of leadership. This stage starts when accountability has been established, progress has been made, and there is trust between the two parties. This one-on-one relationship is focused on passing on valuable knowledge through support, challenge, and appraisal that builds a flexible and strong leader. Downfalls may occur when the leadership style of the coach opposes or suppresses that of the student, either causing conflict or a cookie-cutter alteration. Although coaching should be considered at as many turns the leader takes in their development.

- **Self-directed learning**
  In the final method, the leader is being proactive by challenging and assessing themselves on a scheduled basis. This person will be able to see with more clarity where they still need to improve personally and productively. This method should be an ongoing process on the leadership ladder as you will start noticing how things change before your eyes and how fast you have to move to adapt to it. Lifelong learning is what it takes to access the leadership success we always talk about. The value of formal training is conducive, but if they no longer show interest in learning once situated in an established role, then there will never be space for improvement.

I hope you will understand that taking action by pulling up your socks and asking for permission, advice, or guidance is never a bad thing. Maybe your organization does not feel you are ready to start the process of fine-tuning your development. That does not mean you cannot start being the leader you believe yourself to be now, in this very moment! Without needing the assistance of superiors, you can still learn. Nothing stops you from taking your own initiative.

The internet is a wondrous place, and if you know where to look, you can get all the information that you need without spending a cent. I acknowledge the importance of investing in your future, but by being curious about other methods and various concepts of growth, you can broaden your horizons and replace old notions.

Developing Leadership Skills

Developing the correct skills is no small feat. This is not something that happens overnight (as you might have gathered from the rest of the chapters), and it is something that takes trial and error and a good measure of self-reflected course correction.

To begin developing, you will need to start establishing milestones for yourself in terms of knowledge gathered, relationships built, and professionalism in your field. The responsibilities, skills, and tasks set in place for yourself are what will guide you and teach you how to do things properly.

I do understand that we all have a background that dictates how we handle ourselves with the responsibilities that enter our lives. Some really make it their prerogative to get things done three days ahead of time, while others leave it to the last day. Developing will always mean staying on top of what is important to you and your career, and procrastination is a poisonous apple.

Things happen in life that force us to sacrifice time for one thing over another, but not overindulging and keeping your temperament and overall attitude focused on the game is always advised.

So, what are the actions one needs to take to develop and learn authentically? Here are some pointers:

- Make that mental plan we spoke about earlier. It all starts with a brave purpose.
- Nothing happens without a bit of passion and drive.

- Those around you and ahead of you are influencers of this development.
- All those short, medium, and long-term goals are being routinely assessed.
- Making mistakes and failing are part of the process, learning too.
- Inspiring others is where you shine.

What comes to mind is the inspirational thought which hits the nail on the head when we talk about growth and development. The American author and blogger, Mark Manson, recently wrote on his channel (2021):

> You can't grow muscle without challenging it with greater weight. You can't build emotional resilience without going through hardship and loss. You can't sharpen your mind without challenging your own beliefs and assumptions. Challenging and improving your life requires you to destroy a part of yourself and replace it with a newer, better part of yourself. Therefore, growth is, by definition, painful. (Manson, 2021)

The sentiment here is rather fitting for developing anything in whichever fields your pursuit lies. The momentous realization that finding your true value and your maturity in life comes from exposure. And so, developing your leadership skills requires you to expose yourself to all the weird and wonderful experiences that pepper our lives with joy, sadness, and everything in between.

5

Essential Leadership Skill 01: Communication Skills

Wise men speak because they have something to say; fools because they have to say something.

—Plato

We have all been in that situation where you are attempting to tell a friend about a problem, but they just don't seem to grasp the importance or point, or you are giving a presentation to the board and many confused people are looking back at you. That is what we call miscommunication. It happens to the best of us, and it can complicate even the simplest of messages. Having a basic understanding of what happens when we communicate can teach you to avoid making mistakes.

We currently understand three methods of communication:

1. **The Transmission Model** tells us a message should directly be communicated from the sender (encoder) to the receiver (decoder), without the

need for feedback. This simply cannot hold all the complexities of actual effective communication and impedes many teams.

2. **The Interactive Model** relies on feedback between sender and receiver to allow the one to process that the message was understood. This is not necessarily a bad model, but it does not indicate a full understanding of the message, just the confirmation of receipt.

3. **The Transactional Model** of communication is where constant exchanges of information are involved. Being a far more conducive system to address all the more complex challenges that can come between two communicators by shared meaning and their comprehension of the message.

So, what confuses the action of communication most often? Well, our own subjective lenses are the main reason we might not understand the message. Where an interpretation is given by the sender, but a completely opposite interpretation is made by the receiver.

We pass the ball of communication between us, and every time we touch it, we are molding that message according to our past experiences, the situation in life, current worldview, and systematic beliefs and then passing it back to the other person. Close friends will understand the words used and be able to communicate with more ease while strangers could find difficulty in catching innuendos and semantics used.

So, we can say that communication is one of the most critical functions of a leader. Especially if you are throwing the ball between a whole team of individuals, with all their own perceptions and interpretations of how the task or problem should be solved. There lies the challenge!

And there has never been a better time to improve communication skills than now that the virtual world is getting closer and closer each day. We see that through online meetings and virtual calls between employer and employee, a gap has widened and, unfortunately, at times prevented effective communication. Yes, a screen shows a face, but nothing compares to having a conversation face to face (or should I say, mask to mask) so as to see their body language and detailed facial cues.

"Considering the ongoing globalization and digitalization of work processes, collaborating in digital and virtual teams has become an important aspect of work in many organizations" (Kohntopp & Mccann, 2017). This virtual leader now needs to double the effort put into their team, and work harder to foster better relationships by keeping up to date and getting constant feedback.

Whether this will doom the leadership value or better it by incorporating a more laid-back style and agenda to work-life in the future, that is still unsure. But what is plain to see is that methods of correspondence need to up their game so that efficient and cooperative communication can take place. Misunderstandings need to be addressed by asking yourself, "How can I relate across a platform with more clear and concise messages and requests?"

The aspect of communication having such an effect on what your followers see in you is how you become a more grounded and mature leader. That leader wisely considers what they say and what is said to them. No matter the environmental change, a leader can still guide and encourage through any medium, as long as their methods are clear and calm.

Therefore, you get the idea that this function is rather important and that giving it enough weight in your day-to-day experiences will get you very far.

Why Is It Necessary for Leaders to Have Good Communication Skills?

The encouragement, stimulation, and persuasion you show to others will come back tenfold in co-operation and enhanced outputs. The ineffective communicator will often make the mistake of not speaking and listening with empathy, patience, and honesty. Remembering that "effective communication is an essential component of professional success whether it is at the interpersonal, inter-group, intre-group, organizational, or external level" (Myatt, 2014).

Unfortunately, it can be turned around in the most despicable way, where persuasion is deceitful and disrespectful to the group. It reminds me of the illuminating Turkish proverb: "The forest was shrinking but the trees kept voting for the Axe. For the Axe was clever and convinced the trees that because his handle was made of wood, he was one of them."

Leaders have a duty to uphold communication practices that build morale and increase individuals' motivation. A man can build mountains or break granite with eloquence and appropriate language use, therefore their core responsibility is using that language for the benefit of everyone in their space.

"It has been observed that all the managers or leaders are mostly busy in communicating with one or another while working and spend 70 to 90 percent of their time in a group or team interactions every day" (Luthra & Richa Dahiya, 2015). That is a very big chunk of the day spent talking and bouncing ideas!

What a leader should really be focused on is adopting the correct mindset while discussing sometimes straightforward tasks and sometimes sensitive topics. Sure, you speak all day, but with what motif, with what intent? You want to be able to interact with all kinds of personalities and be the middle ground for stability between them. A leader does not justify their communication to change someone's ideas, but to align them with their own.

Dealing with arguments is arguably (excuse the pun) the main reason why a leader should adopt brilliant communication skills. Two points to consider are:

1. In every argument, you are not necessarily right.
2. You are not diminished if you change your beliefs during an argument.

Human beings get carried away by emotion and conviction. When a leader expresses their interest in others' convictions, then a moment is shared. The follower will build respect for a leader who possesses the ability to look further than what is presented, and acknowledge what is really being conveyed. This is something that takes time and practice, of course.

When a leader can ruminate on people's reasons, standpoints, and opinions before jumping straight into a frame of disagreement, then connections are forged by the simple attempt to relate.

Forget all about the "yes, but..." viewpoint that often gets interjected into a conversation. A great leader never succumbs to their motivations first because they allow for the speaker to finish their conversation and portray their thoughts completely. Leaders need to understand that they bring more to the table by listening, rather than speaking.

Remember I mentioned keeping a journal to record your thoughts? Well, this is where that becomes practical. Your ability to keep track of ideas and feelings is critical to your overall improvement. Therefore, start small and the more you do it every day (preferably in the mornings and evenings) the more you get used to relying on the physical act of writing to ruminate.

Strong Communication Skills to Develop as a Leader

Now that you have the idea of why communication is at the forefront of strong leadership, I would like to give you some pointers on how you can develop your own communication skills to better your environment.

A strong leader will apply the following to their style of leadership:

Listen With Ears, Eyes, and Gut

Communication is more than just words and when you learn to see those three separate aspects of communication independently, you are actually seeing the whole picture. For example, when your colleague enters your office, their eyes are lowered, their body posture is closed and cold, this is immediately a red flag of something serious going on. When they say read the room, they mean it!

An employee or peer will automatically show you the signals that something is not in sync. Either they use their vocal capacities by telling you straight up how they feel or through body language. Either way, your duty is to be aware of these aspects, take into account all the signs that someone is in a bad place mentally or physically, and that by asking and engaging with them on a human level, they will open up. The same courtesy should be done by them in turn. You are not the only one allowed to question. If you are down and out, just having a terrible day, and someone asks how you are, you do not dismiss them because they could not possibly understand, but rather allow them to see that you can be unsure and have bad days too. You thank them for taking the time to ask, and you look them in the eyes and appreciate that tender moment, immediately building trust and respect!

Take the Time to Understand

Involve your attention in other people's input with as much interest as you would like to be understood in turn. The number one key point here is validation. Avoid getting carried away with responding and filling the silence with words. Instead, use that time to ponder on the message they are relating to you. Summarize your thoughts clearly beforehand, and when they have finished talking, you can express (kindly and empathetically) what you have understood. It is a helpful trick to respond with questions on the matter.

For example, a person has opened their hearts to you about how miserable they are at this company. By asking them more about what they have stated, like, "So you are saying that you are unhappy about working here due to tension with colleagues?" or, "I hear you, but tell me, is this something you have been feeling for some time now?" When requesting more in-depth detail from their side and finding the hidden premise, you can solve the riddle of subtle communication and elevate the importance of the other person.

The Effects of Perceptual Awareness Filters

They alter how we react, confront, and doubt situations. It is your own personal preconception that you are fighting for every day, not the elemental truth. Every other person on earth has their own that they let guide them and steer them to good or bad choices. So again, I require you to always be in the "asking mode." Show curiosity for their worldview, find a middle ground, something which you can both agree on, and work your way up from there.

For example, by asking, "Why do you feel that way?" or, "Tell me more about that experience", you never assume your perception is the objective truth. You will automatically calm the whole situation down and hopefully, both will learn something new about each other.

Be Specific and Know What Impact Your Words Have

Being brief and clear about what you have to say can ease unnecessary double meaning or misinterpreted requests. You would want to learn how to get to the higher points of the conversation, to the real meat of it, by cutting to the chase. This is a two-way street, where both communicators understand when it's time to speak with meaning and intent, and when it's time to speak with ease and neutrality. These different situations have two very different outcomes and require another type of energy.

By showing that you can get to the point faster by de-weeding all the superfluous words that sometimes get in the way, you can create more time for actioned results. Receive an issue and come back with an answer that clarifies a space, consents for input, and compels action.

Be Sure You Know Exactly What You're Talking About

In situations when someone does not have technical command over what they are attempting to say, this conveys a lack of maturity and substance, especially for the leader. Make sure you know all aspects of your field and show a keen interest in what others say if they know more. If you are not clued up on the full breakdown of what is transpiring, ask more questions or keep quiet. Secret students are those that never forget where they fell short. They work it out in isolation so that tomorrow they don't look and sound unsure. By always getting feedback on your own skills at hand, you are also showing readiness to grow.

You must have been exposed to interviews or speeches at some point in your life from people who you admire and aspire to be one day. By critically evaluating their words, their mannerisms, and their pacing you can start analyzing the patterns of successful communication. Instead of noting exactly what they say, assess how they say these sentences in accordance with the message. Inflections of voice, pauses for effect, repetition, and rhetoric questions all have their purpose. Therefore, sit down and write your perceptions on their conversationalist talent and incorporate it into your plan and process.

Great Leaders' Secret Strategies to Effective Communication

The first rule to great leaders activating outstanding communication is to adapt their leadership style to their communication style according to the different situations that appear in their space. Remember, rigidity is death. To always be evolving and trying new things, you can learn more about others and, in turn, yourself.

The leader evolves their communication to fit the situations. It's feeling what kind of communication that space needs and implementing it with grace and ease. You cannot possibly use the same communication in a board meeting with lawyers, as you would with your colleagues in the canteen.

Great leaders know the power of their voice, of their stories, and of their quotes. Here are some strategies that great leaders use to enhance their communication:

- **They speak like leaders**
  They know what they want, and they know how to get across to people for it to happen. They evoke meaning in each sentence and practice in front of a mirror or with people they trust so they can get concrete feedback. To convey confidence, great leaders find surety in knowing that they sound persuasive, accountable, and most of all, relatable. They use approaches like rhetoric, speech, metaphors, and the rule of three while pounding

the message just at the right time to entice the audience.

- **They are enthusiastic, especially to listen**
  This is surely something that you now understand to be important when dealing with people, but great leaders show (really show) that they care what other people think. They listen with focus and interest. They are enthusiastic about being around people who have input in the game and whose feelings and thoughts add tremendous value to the team. Some like to make notes during a conversation or immediately afterward, so as to reflect even further on what was said.

- **They tell intriguing (and relevant) stories**
  Telling better stories with more structure and flow can really up the game. Great leaders have a wonderful way of mining their experiences and past actions so as to come together into a tale that brings focus, emotion, and a central moral to the story. It certainly engages the audience around them and unites them further into the deeper message. Learning by watching others is one way to improve, but also taking public speaking courses can help fine-tune this skill.

- **They do not up-talk**
  This basically means that the inflection of the voice rises at the end of the sentence, making it almost seem questioning. This confuses people and it is a bad habit many don't know they have. Practice by recording yourself speaking, writing down sentences that sound inflected, and focusing on the syllables that need to be turned down a notch. Then

re-teach yourself how to pronounce them effectively by focusing on using the word correctly.

- **They know who agrees with them and who doesn't**
  It is imperative to understand that life requires conflict, contrary beliefs, and opinions of all sorts. Without that, we wouldn't push further for the truth. But these leaders certainly are not naïve about the people who don't agree with them and what they say. This is about accepting that others have the right to feel however they want and communicating that with etiquette and respect is very important.

- **They write**
  Indeed, everything they feel, experience, reject, or are confused about gets transcribed from their inner thoughts to paper. It is an incredible way to be a more effective communicator when you can read your own thoughts and evaluate how to convey them to others later in a more coordinated and conclusive way.

- **They are aware that they are not talking to a group, but many individuals**
  This comes more into play when we talk about large presentations where they would have to address a room filled with many people, for example. Stage fright, insecurity, doubt, all these emotions are under the spotlight. But great leaders know one secret here: they are relaying the message as they go to each person. Each individual who is listening to this speech has their own perceptual hearing. Whether it be a conference or a small board

meeting, they bring a personal aspect to each person sitting there.

- **They know the power of humor**
  A laugh or two, a comical situation, and sometimes an embarrassing moment can be a fantastic way to break the ice. This needs to be especially well balanced and used in exceptional situations, like meeting new team members or selling a new idea. I understand that not everyone has a fast whip on humorous talk, but by smiling, laughing, and engaging in other people's humor, it can help the leader evaluate where they can improve their own. The leader needs to learn where they can let their hair down and relate and when they need to be the serious boss who gets things done.

Keep dissecting all the various aspects of your communication style with keen interest. Watch others do their thing so you can improve your own body language, tone of voice, and words used. Never push for characteristics that do not come naturally to you but rather find comfort in elevating those that you feel better your intrinsic style.

6

Essential Leadership Skill 02: Interpersonal Skills

We live in a society obsessed with public opinion. But leadership has never been about popularity.

—Marco Rubio

It is imperative that a leader understands the concept of interpersonal skills in regard to being a better employer or a better mentor in their fields. The workplace is evolving rapidly and more diversity means learning more about others.

The great inspirational speaker and author Simon Sinek explained this very well in his TED Talk back in 2017 about the power of empathy. He mentioned how embarrassed he was to have to explain to top executives about trust and cooperation in a business setting. He recognized a terribly large gap between the employee and the employer, where a deeper understanding of aligning leaders and followers' perspectives was not considered.

A good leader needs to have two things: empathy and perspective. These can be sometimes forgotten in the rush of being in a certain position in the company. An employer or manager will tend to lose sight of what is most important at that level of expertise. Not them using that position to control the charge they have on others, but putting that control in giving charge to others. Focusing on who needs the guidance and mentorship, instead of focusing on the figures and their own responsibilities.

The transition of being a junior employer gaining the ranks by going to more training courses or furthering their studies so they may be a lot better at their jobs is the basic concept of climbing the ladder, correct? When you have proven yourself to be proficient at your job, then you could possibly be promoted. Some other junior will take that place from you and now you will be in charge of managing them.

Now, an issue may develop when we see that the junior is not getting the same grooming as the manager got back in their day. The junior employee might not know the exact tricks of the trade, the certain aspects of the job, which might infuriate the manager and bring negative impacts to the relationship. When the person who was responsible for the job is now in charge of the people who are responsible for it, a misunderstanding of the role and reason behind the transition becomes the main objective. Confrontation and irritation build and build.

I would like to show you how you can remove that negative resonance and find the singularity of your transition. You need to be the leader that led you. If you feel that you were trained, mentored, and groomed well into the leader you are today, you cannot possibly expect your juniors to reach the same goals without that guidance.

The Impact of Your Interpersonal Skills on Your Leadership

When you spend more time at the office to help those who look up to you, they are recognizing that you are not just responsible for tasks being completed, but for the people who do that job and do it properly. Practice that personal sacrifice and care.

The number of customers, the maximization of shareholders' value, and the product development are secondary and third to the value of the people who make it all possible at the end of the day. There would be no company if there was no one to do the nitty-gritty of the job, the step-by-step basic work to move the company forward every fiscal year. So by thinking that the world the leader revolves around is based on the above-mentioned aspects of a company, then the company will most probably have a fast hire and fire strategy that most certainly negatively impacts the organization as a whole.

Where we see transformation in employees, the most is through learning to create a safe and accommodating environment for the best performance. This environment, in turn, is both a physical and interpersonal space. What social benefit will you gain by asking the people around you what they need, when they need it, and why they need it? Everything!

How do your interpersonal skills show in your leadership styles? Let us look at this a little more in-depth, shall we?

- **The verbal and non-verbal communication**
  As we touched on in chapter 5, the act of being more of an active listener and communicator all-around can increase the chances of a team running like clockwork. The verbal can be more direct where your voice tone and the select usage of words, but the non-verbal can be a whole lot more meaningful. Being cognizant of looking people in the eyes, showing that you are listening, and having a body posture that allows for people to be open towards you is essential. Deviate from crossing your arms in front of your chest and rather keep them hanging at your sides or on your hips. The open and approachable dress sense can do wonders, too. All leadership styles will require a thorough spoon full of this subtle art of communication.

  I would like you to think carefully about scenarios from your past experience when communicating with friends, family, and other acquaintances. Think about how your emotions have at times been irrational and that maybe something was said out of turn. Make note of the three most dominant emotions you feel in a day and what triggers you towards the negative ones. Take note of what you project onto others as well and note how you can improve your own emotional output to connect to more people rather than, in some cases, turn them away.

- **Your empathy levels**
  This can be terribly difficult to master, but to really be able to put yourself in the shoes of others means that you will never fall short of having someone who looks up to you. It is such a core characteristic

that appeals to those around you, that it stands very close to the top of the list of attributes some of the best leaders in our history ever had.

Your perceptions could change if you simply practice relating more and dissociating less. The next time you feel that you could possibly never be able to understand someone else's side, just force yourself to remember that the beauty in this world is the fact that we are all different, unique, and fragile beings. We all deserve a chance to exist honestly and freely in this world, and the opportunity to relate more can change the situation around for the better. Rather ask more questions about their own reasonings. Let them explain themselves so you might grasp their point, their justifications, and their thoughts better.

- **Your negotiation skills**
  With great power comes great responsibility, this we know. And in its own important way, negotiating strategically in tough decision-making scenarios is a power. The main point of this aspect is to find a win-win solution to the conflict or discussion. Your persuasion, planning, strategizing, and, most importantly, cooperation with a message you wish to deploy is what you need to focus on. You will have to adjust this soft skill depending on the environment (formal or informal) and what the final outcome of this negotiation will bring.

Jot down what your opening point is in a discussion, how you would keep timing in the conversations, how much commitment you have in the outcome, and how actively you listen to those around you. Practice by writing scripts of yourself talking to your peers, and find a conclusion where you always have a silver lining on both sides. The leader is required to prepare with dedication before the time, and always be on top of the situation.

Key Interpersonal Skills of a Good Leader

Start by caring about human beings. These soft skills of leadership are one of the basal principles to effective teamwork and being a decent individual overall!

The following skills will elevate your leadership when implemented accurately:

- **Bringing confidence to your team**
  Instilling a sense of empowerment in the team or group of people around you is probably the first rule to being a well-adjusted leader. It is critical that a sense of ownership of their own skills and influence in the corporation or team is communicated. Implementing this strategy is a 50/50 exercise. You give them the opportunity to shine, and they take that cue to be more than just a number.

- **Praise where necessary**
  Yes, praise is great. We are fully aware of the benefits of the praise. But the praise needs to be tactical too. You need to be able to read the people around you and their specific needs at that moment. You praise when things are going well, but you also praise when things go badly. Meaning, you see the error the person made, but you begin by telling them where they went right, and then touching on how they can avoid the mistake again.

- **Show trust and value honesty**
  You want to be trusted and respected. Everybody does. But that starts with you. You have the power now to instill more trust in the team by showing how vulnerable you can be as well. If you are not human in your dealings with the people that effectively act on your choices and decisions, resentment and eventual hatred could boil to the surface. You being transparent and clear about what you want, how you feel, and the true nature of your concern will automatically give them the key to do the same, which is precisely what you need. Their valuable honesty and trust that when they do have something to say that is not politically correct, you are able to relate and laugh with them.

- **Be a more selfless leader**
  We spoke about parenthood earlier, and this aspect is where we see how your concern in their inclusion in the team might sometimes mean that you get the brunt for being more selfless than what is usually expected by the manager. You are one of them. You have been in their shoes, and you know what kind of leader you would have liked to have at your side when things didn't go according to plan. By being more selfless with your time, your persona, your image of mentor, then the credit is due to them. You stand back and let the praise be for others. Even though you might have contributed to 80% of the results, the praise stays on their side.

- **Include general wellness aspects**
  It is a fact that the company or team should be ready when they jump on board the program. They should come into the office or open that zoom call

in top form, peak performance, just brimming with excitement and positivity. That is ideal, right? But what happens when someone cannot show that face right now? How do you confront the personal concept of wellness in your team? By applying the above principles, of course! You tell them about what wellness is to you, and how this can be a factor to consider if you want to get to work on time, do what needs to be done and go home feeling accomplished. Wellness of mind, spirit, and body can increase your love for the job by being balanced and centralized.

- **Manage conflict**
  We spoke about this before, but it is a biggie. Great leaders are also extensively emotional, but they manage it with nerves of steel and experience. If you can summon the character that is needed when things start getting heated and people express unhappiness and unfulfillment, then you will need to step into the role of mediator. This is not just between members of your team, but even when you are the possible reason for dissatisfaction or friction. You will need to find a way to ready your character for evaluation and dig deeper into the followers' reasons too. Being calm and concise while open to input are the agendas you need to adopt when conflict shows up.

Improving Your Interpersonal Skills

We are not born into this world with the purpose of being perfect. It is perfect to simply strive to be a better person than you were yesterday, and that is where I would like you to orientate your mindset when it comes to interpersonal relationships. We now understand that communication is a central role in enhancing relationships therefore, it needs to be incorporated heavily into your team and their individual needs.

There are six aspects that could assist you in improving these skills, some of which are equal in weight in other chapters in this book. The conglomerate of leadership often entails an interwoven set of skills that feature in more than one leadership style and model.

1. **Cross-cultural training**
    This is the ability to illuminate the need for diversity and inclusion. Take the time to do the training that brings the world to you. You want to learn how to involve yourself better in this multi-cultural environment we all live in today. Whether it's a global team or the company works with foreign investors, this all still requires an overview of cultures, religions, ethics, and race. You also want to be aware of who is married, who has children, who has what schooling, and where they are from. This means getting to know your team with more care and acknowledgment. By this, you can find that you relate better to them, you find commonalities and likes, and you begin to develop into the caring leader they all need.

2. **Maintaining relationships**
    Starting a relationship can be the easy part but maintaining them is another story altogether. Constantly working on each person in an allocation style, you make sure those few minutes of conversation are not just about performance, but about them, and their lives and loves outside of

work. Find ways to maintain these relationships every so often, if possible, by keeping up to date in your diary with those you have not interacted with meaningfully in that week and focus on them for the following week. It might seem silly at first, but the reward of seeing how the followers react to your interest in a constant manner will put a light in your eyes.

3. **Practice active listening**
   Earlier we spoke about active listening in the skill of communication. This aspect fits right in with the interpersonal idea of leadership. Again, by staying focused, keeping eye contact, looking for non-verbal cues, and judging less, the conversation can become a two-way expression. The leader responds only when the person has completely finished speaking. They ask more questions rather than stating their opinion mid-talk and attempt to summarize their ideas before you vocalize them.

4. **Recognize the traits and expertise in each follower**
   The leader sees potential. That is their job! They use that time to come up with more tactical ways to include others in the decision-making process and bring out each individual's natural skill set in certain arenas. This can help the leader delegate better and give more praise to improved and pro-active behavior.

5. **Control the outlook by including positivity and emotional intelligence (EI)**
   We spoke about the concept of EI earlier, and this is no exception to the rule. If you learn to master this by re-assessing yourself at each turn, then,

over time, this will hopefully become a facet of leadership that you can enjoy and bring to your whole entire life. As mentioned, you need to be open and empathetic, so find a way to relate to situations with clarity, kindness, and awareness of others.

The Interpersonal Leader

The interpersonal, intrapersonal, and professional leadership styles affect each other independently to bring about a brilliant leader. If the person knows when to use the skill for each scenario and uses it well, then there is the magic!

This leader will be driven to ground their own emotions, those of others, and be fully aware of what professional environment they wish to embrace. When the leader reflects an attitude that is calm, cohesive, and controlled, they instill clarity to the followers around them. Their recognition of how they affect others first and then how others affect them in the organization or team is what makes them so perceptive and accommodating.

You will now need to incorporate personal exercises for yourself so that you learn to be the interpersonal leader they need.

1. Study your followers by understanding what their expectations are and where their prejudices lie. Who are they? What theme do they encompass? Where can I relate to them? What skills do they enjoy accessing?
2. Observe the physical and emotional barriers that can impede communication and interpersonal development. Do I encompass an open attitude?

Are my own personal barriers preventing connections? Does the environment promote interpersonal development?

3. <u>Change</u> how you approach individuals by using your own personal and social skills to guide your followers into a work pattern that is healthy and productive. Am I emotionally intelligent about conflict? Do I express my view for change and improvement in an understanding way? Do I embrace feedback?

It takes time and effort to know when to use the empathetic side and when not to. The fine line of mentorship, just like in parenthood, does not necessarily require you to be best friends with them. You simply need to guide them in the correct course of action and decision-making. "People still subscribe to the pyramid model of leadership, where the king sits at the top and is supported by legions of team members who strive to please. Instead, true leadership is like an inverted pyramid with the entire organization relying on a single leader to support their efforts" (Meyers, 2016). Their needs are equal or more important than your own in essence, and their actions are a reflection of your honest and clear support, not your friendship.

By all means, stay on friendly terms, but going too far and confiding in them too soon can cause more conflict than staying neutral to the party. Let them find friendship in their peers, in their teammates, and in their colleagues by giving them that space to do so comfortably.

The thought of having to keep certain aspects of your job under wraps and implementing your leadership style on a 'need to know basis' is initially beneficial, but then can become problematic when trust and honor are broken amongst the followers. Yes, you have commitments and responsibilities that are not on the shoulders of your followers, but that does not isolate you from your choice on how to approach them together.

7

Essential Leadership Skill 03: Problem Solving & Decision-Making Skills

Innovation distinguishes between a leader and a follower.

—Steve Jobs

There are two ways to play the game of business and the game of people. You can either choose for it to be built on a finite system of rules, where there is a winner and a loser. Or you can choose to adhere to the infinite system of simply playing to stay in the game.

The first is what we would see in the standard games of sports and war, where a match or battle crowns one a winner and the other a loser. This is finite and rules apply. The organization or team usually are focusing most of their attention on how to beat the opposition, how to outwit and outmaneuver them.

The infinite game is a lot more conducive to bigger and better things in the professional world. By improving the experience within the company rather than being obsessed with who the competition is, how many customers you have, and what your employee number is, you are showing others that you are not competing against anyone but yourself. Zooming into the idea of how to improve from within and staying in the game.

This is how decision-making and problem solving encompasses that. You make decisions based on the environment and the set of ideals the company has for the future. You find solutions that solve what? You bring people together to brainstorm for whose benefit?

It is essential that the leader has a clear vision of the whole picture. That they break up that picture into smaller, manageable pieces and take each with careful consideration.

What comes to mind when I think about great leadership decisions is the inspirational book written by US Navy Captain L. David Marquet. *Turn the Ship Around!* is a story about self-discovery, accumulated tension, and the ability to make the tough decisions count. It is commonly known that authoritarian leadership styles fit best in the commanding seat of lieutenants and captains of war fleets, but here, we see how one person makes a decision that turns the standard rules of autocratic leadership on its head.

David made the error to assume that his credibility as a leader was based on his intelligence and know-how of each submarine he commanded, learning the system of the machine fully and commanding his crew by total knowledge. The chink in the armor came when at the last minute, he was stationed to a different submarine, the *Santa Fe*, which he hadn't had enough time to study before departure. Fearing a loss in credibility and trust, he did not mention to the crew (who had been on board a long while) that he was not technically competent on this older model. He decided to get on with it anyway, trusting his orders to be enough.

It started well until a test run was made on day three, where the nuclear power cores were turned off so the crew may start their standard drill sequence. David, standing at the helm and assuming that this vessel had the same modalities as the newer model he had poured over, barked orders to the first officer beside him to apply specific settings to the power to change the route by some degrees. The first officer relayed the same order to the second officer who was meant to physically make the changes, but nothing happened. The captain asked why they were delaying the maneuver and not adhering to the command, and the first officer simply stated that this model of the vessel did not have that setting he requested. The captain asked the officer why he repeated the order to his second in command if he knew that this ship didn't have that setting and the first officer's answer triggered something with David. The first officer beside him nervously replied that because he was following orders and that was his duty, he had no other choice.

David didn't fully know the environment he was in and he didn't know the crew well enough to have a more concrete relationship. He was off his game as a leader because he expected the crew to know how to operate the machine correctly even with his incorrect orders. David wrote, "What goes on in your workplace every day that reinforces the notion that the guys at the top are the leaders and everyone else is simply to follow? I was startled to find that this was pervasive on *Santa Fe*," (L. David Marquet, 2013, p. 56). This put a spanner in the works because he couldn't make the right decisions to ensure the safety of the crew and the mission. Therefore, David made the choice to manage the environment differently and allow the team to make choices of their own due to their better knowledge of the vessel. And it changed everything.

Top men and women have all the authority, but sometimes none of the information. This is a tornado that can kill everything in sight if not controlled and assessed appropriately. David understood that leaving the chain of command as permission-based was folly, which required him to give sound orders with the knowledge he did not have. So he solved this problem with a tactical maneuver that turned the ship around. He allowed the sailors to rather have responsibility for their own performance on the *USS Santa Fe*, not on him giving individual orders. More responsibility was given to the officers to make deliberate and conscious choices of their own over the whole season at sea. They would not request permission but rather ask for the support of their own decision towards the captain. They would tell him what they planned, he would discuss it with them, and they would get the job done. This form of supportive leadership bloomed, and they eventually became the highest-rated crew in naval history. Nine of the officers on board the submarine eventually ended up captaining their own crew later on (which is terribly rare in most cases).

This model of support, encouragement and passive delegation does better to build new leaders rather than a rigid and outdated model, which requires staying in rank and never having the opportunity to deviate and question. This leader-to-leader model was exceptional in this particular environment, and he saw that only later after he had made the mistake of overestimating himself and underestimating the crew.

Therefore, I tell you one thing out of this. Leadership does not mean never making mistakes, it means making these mistakes and learning from them together with better decision-making and incorporated problem-solving. It makes leaders prime and shine in the most outstanding manner.

Problem-Solving and Decision-Making Hand in Hand

First and foremost, let me break down the concepts of problem-solving and decision-making in the respective power they hold.

Problem-solving involves the identification of solutions to a rising situation or issue at hand. It is a part of the decision-making process and is most often processed as the time spent on the issue increases. The more we know about the problem, the better decisions can be implemented.

While decision-making is using the judgment one has on the problem itself and standing strong on them to bring confidence and surety to the team. These decisions will become more complex as your position as a leader becomes more critical to the team. To follow steps methodically and fix the problem, a leader needs to:

1. Use their problem-solving skills to uncover a brilliant solution that came from smart decisions made and the opportunity you gave others to tackle it too.
2. Understand if the solution is viable for the problem that is in front of them.
3. Make a final decision on what the following moves should be to action that solution.

The betterment in one skill set does not necessarily mean that the other follows suit, even if they are simpatico. One can be overlooked too often and become a huge downfall. For instance, you make plenty of small decisions throughout the week but have not managed to solve the underlying problem. Are you always plugging holes in the ship but not knowing where the true problem lies?

In a contrary situation (which is where we see followers most discontent), we see the person has knowledge of the problem and how to solve it, but not have the power to make the decisions that could solve it. Do you have the recognition to make that choice? Do you let others share input which leaves more space for answers and solutions? Are you allowing for more inclusivity in problem-solving?

Finally, critical thinking is a key that can unlock all of this in one go. Applying more logic and sense to solving the problem, exploring new ideas, and questioning those that have been around for a long time, can bring innovation and a breath of fresh air to the sometimes stagnant scenes of 'finding better ways to do things'. Your research and study of the people, the environment, and the issue in its complexities can create space for others to assist as you now know what attributes your followers have that can grasp the specific issue with ease.

Therefore, the leader needs to seriously consider what decision they can make now under whichever circumstances are available to them. They make small progress each day by making good decisions that contribute to the overall issue. Small bite sizes later will accumulate to a solution. Be a leader who makes the best out of every situation thrown at you and attempt (as you grow) to incorporate these lessons into your life.

First Principles of Thinking

Do you remember when you were a child (or you have one of your own) and you used to grind your parents down by asking questions about everything that you were curious about? Questions are always at the forefront of childhood with sometimes silly and sometimes profound inquiries like, why does this happen? How is it made? Why can't I have it? What does this do?

Children have an innate way to get their honest feelings shown by simply asking more transparent questions. By asking for the basic reality of the issue in an easy-to-understand manner. This is what pivoted scientists to recognize how first principles can contribute to decision-making tremendously.

Why do they call it the first principle of thinking? Well, Aristotle described the first principle as "the first basis for which a thing is known" (Clear, 2017), meaning that it is required to be questioned and researched more in-depth. It demands an explanation. It systematically doubts everything until only the purest truth remains. This can also be termed as the Cartesian doubt.

Why do you think we grow up to be so cynical and edgy after school and no longer question like we did? That is most likely related to the educational system around the world that has stifled curiosity and prevented us from finding wonder in so many things. Perhaps we can train ourselves to step back and remember how to ask like a child to get answers that rock the core.

More clear cut answers and solutions to problem-solving in many environments can be discovered only once you understand that nothing is ever truly known until you start:

1. Dissecting the problem into manageable parts. Find what needs to be questioned and what assumptions have been made about this common issue. Use critical thinking in identifying these conjectures and why they exist.
2. Bringing to your aid a plentiful number of pure questions toward the problem. Honestly and transparently question the fundamental origin of the system, what evidence tells you about the problematic situation, and un-connect the facts from the assumptions.
3. Never forgetting the mission starts by using the answers you discovered from the relentless investigation. Finding or creating that new solution that fits well with (hopefully) two or three issues at once is where you want to be.

I have an exercise for you: Picture an image with an animal in it. A photo, a painting, an image on your computer. You see the image as a whole, but what is within that image that can be separated and analyzed in isolation? You have the animal, you have the background environment, the grass, the trees. You have the sky and the objects within it. These can be classified, separated, analyzed, and, most importantly, questioned. You can classify the variant colors present, where they group more and where they group less. You can furthermore break down the image into something minuscule, like the number of pixels present within.

This very process of machine learning classification is an incredible tool to accomplish feats of innovation and creation that some of the greatest minds of the 21st century preach.

Keep in mind the knowledge of step 1, where the more you address looking for core aspects of each problem that comes your way, the more you start seeing how many of those manageable parts share similar characteristics with other manageable parts of a separate issue entirely. That leads you to eventually start seeing how combining the characteristics of one aspect to another (where we find most inventions sprout from) brings a whole new innovative solution to the light.

You have to build an experiential knowledge of the problem, so facing it again is done with far more ease and elegance. And then, with more expertise, find better ways to manage problems that arise and implement great strategies that transcend and allow it to no longer be labeled a problematic situation.

Inversion: Thinking Forward and Backward

There is an interesting quote by the philanthropist and business mogul Charlie Munger that helps us launch the concept for this chapter. He says, "All I want to know is where I am going to die, so I'll never go there" (Hicham

Fleihan, 2021). This can be translated into a method of thinking that requires you to change your viewpoint. Instead of asking how you can win in life, how about you rather ask how you can avoid a loss. Interesting, right?

Imagine you are a big-time manager for a football club. You have worked and focused all your team's attention on making sure that goals are scored, that the skills and talent present quantifies to a win. On match day, your opponent (who might be lower on the log) annihilates you because they did something very different from what you expected. Rather than focus on how to beat the opponent with offensive skill, they most likely asked themselves how they could prevent goals from ever reaching their nets in the first place. They placed a lot of energy in defense, rather than attack which proved valuable, and named them winners. A simple strategy alteration that required inversion thinking.

Now, this is a super powerful tool in solving complex problems that might not have the simplest of answers, to begin with. Just like with the first principles, I ask you to clear your mind from the usual patterns of thought. I ask you to peek your head outside of that proverbial box and see what lies around you. So many opportunities to evaluate and question methods that have been around for decades and find clever ways to beat the system.

Let me equip you with some questions and points that will come in handy when implementing this new tool of thinking:

1. Establish by writing down (remember the trusty pen and paper) all the aspects that frequently see negative light in and around your circle:

- The continuous decline in sales.
- The lack of good reviews and feedback from customers.
- The uninterest of employees in meetings and group workshops.

2. Evaluate how these issues keep popping up:
   - Are you following an age-old system to grow revenue?
   - Are you not assessing customer satisfaction in more detail?
   - Are your presentations boring and time-consuming?

3. Reverse those questions to put more emphasis on what the company might be doing wrong:
   - How can we make the sales drop over a period of time?
   - How can we ignore the customers' needs?
   - How can we bring even more boredom into our company meetings?

4. The answers that appear will be the catalyst for change by doing the exact opposite to what is stipulated:
   - By not adhering to the more eco-conscious worldview and market trend.
   - By ignoring the value of the brand or product to that of the customer.
   - By never thinking about the audience and only about the statistics.

Now, by imagining what you shouldn't be doing in these instances, you can learn what you can do not to win, but not to lose! The art of doing the opposite can alter a thought pattern and bring about results that were aimed for but never reached.

By focusing on what you shouldn't be doing, you can automatically find yourself doing some things right naturally. It can be counterintuitive when conventional wisdom is required for fast-paced solutions. Will you want to achieve success or avoid failure? It is more valuable to know when to use these practices and when not to? Reason with yourself and every intricacy that enters your space.

Law of Parsimony: Simplifying Solutions

We spoke in the introduction to this book about the concept of choice. That the more options available, the more confusion and stress are exhibited. With the idea of simplification, we stand to see that the most basic solutions, the simplest of solutions that are already there for the taking, are usually the most viable way out.

Let's say you are in a life and death situation. Options are everywhere, but what is the fastest and most direct way to survive? Will you be sitting there developing a complex plan, or will you look for the simplest option? The human body and nature all around us are great examples of parsimony. The best solution is usually the simplest one, and it works like a charm!

This theory is derived from principles of scientific thinking of the late Medieval Age, where looking for observed facts meant keeping the hypothesis as simple as possible.

The law of parsimony is also termed Occam's razor (deriving from the 14th-century friar William Ockham. Yes, the spelling went off course at some stage!), re-inventing the law of economy by basically stating that "You gain nothing by complicating an explanation without some corresponding increase in its explanatory power" (Ball, 2016). This means that bringing in more variables to the problem will only cause it to become more complex, which is the opposite of what you need.

The 13th-century Italian philosopher Thomas Aquinas reasons with it perfectly by saying, "If a thing can be done adequately by means of one, it is superfluous to do it by means of several; for we observe that nature does not employ two instruments [if] one suffices" (Baker, 2016).

Paying attention to the characteristics of the tool you use, again, makes much sense. This tool does not make the problem better, per se, but it certainly might make it more useful. If you desire to get to the bare bones of an explanation, then this is a possible method. Sure, we have seen over the many centuries of scientific critical thought that the simplest of reasonings are sometimes faulty and that the underlying issue turns out to be far more complex and intricate. But in our context of leadership and understanding the concepts of solving puzzles that plague our success, then this simplifying method might be the holy grail.

Many top-notch companies have adapted this to their business model. You see this approach consistently in tech companies that require better methods to interface with customers. People prefer clean lines, clear concepts that can allow them to get the job done in the easiest and least time-consuming way.

The true issue comes in when we ask not how problem-solving can assist the business, but how this tool can help encourage others to problem-solve too. We know now that you don't just want to be a manager, a pointer of fingers, a walking talking signature. You want to connect and inspire those who surround you. I would like to take you back to the inversion method, where we learned how to ask not just what something is, but also what it is not.

Leadership is not entirely about motivation, we find that it is best seen when it is about allowing your followers to motivate themselves. You can take a horse to the water, but you cannot make it drink. Therefore, by simplifying how you communicate to your team, you can give them the opportunity to see the path and, therefore, motivate themselves to find the solution. You build that environment that is conducive to individual thought and brings the inner leader out in junior employees as well.

Comprehend how motivation in your organization can revolve around three factors: logic, emotion, and time. You have to appeal to people's logic for them to be emotionally invested in the project, and you have to appeal to their emotions for there to be a sufficient amount of time to be spent facilitating and making decisions based on how they feel about it.

More Mental Models to Help You Make Decisions

Alright, so we have addressed some of the top methods to tackle the sometimes paralyzing effects of not knowing how to make better, cleaner, and faster decisions that positively influence your leadership style and the organizations in which you work.

What we know is that these mental models assist in applying a framework that allows you to make decisions very quickly, without having all that information ahead of time. The intensive detective work is eliminated and distractions are removed. This allows you to get a hell of a lot more out of your day and be more productive with your time.

I would like to show you two more models that can help you assess further what these decisions made can consequently become and what reaction they have on the business and the team.

- **The downstream effect**
  This judges whether your decisions will have a positive or negative recourse in the second, third, or fourth-order of consequences. Let me explain. Humans have the innate concern to focus first on the immediate consequence of their decision, the first-order consequence. For example, we are aware that exercise initially feels pretty crap. After a full workout, you are sweating, achy, and seriously judging your fitness level. This is a first-order consequence. The second and third-order will be increased fitness, better sleep patterns, a more muscled physique, etc. We don't appreciate these until they appear because we have a real hard time practicing looking long term.

  Start by taking that pen and paper and drawing a grid-like schematic with all the options that you see to be available. Then in each grid, apply what consequences will appear in 10 minutes, 10 days, and in 10 months to that decision made. This will allow you to consider and compare these answers to make more direct and useful decisions.

- **The hard choice model**
  Now I'd like to ask you to draw a graph with four quadrants within it. The y-axis (the vertical axis) determines from zero how easy to how hard it is to compare these options. The x-axis (the horizontal axis), on the other hand, determines from zero how low to how high the impact will be on the options made. In each quadrant, you will apply:

  1. The <u>No Brainer</u> choice, which is the easiest to compare (for instance accepting free tickets to a concert is a no brainer) and has the lowest impact.
  2. The next approach is the <u>Apples Versus Oranges</u> choice, which is harder to compare (for instance, choosing to have dinner at your favorite restaurant or choosing the one your friend mentioned), but still in a relatively low impact zone.
  3. Following that, we assess the <u>Big Choice</u> category, which implies that it might be easier to compare the options like the No Brainer, but the impact is still rather high due to the heavier consequences of the choice.
  4. Lastly, the <u>Hard Choice</u> category is the highest of comparisons and the highest of impacts, which requires sensible research time spent to make the decision.

Therefore, what we can judge from the designs you have just sketched of each model of decision-making is that decisions can indeed be categorized by different weights of variables. Depending on what importance they hold, and what impact they make, you can decide in a more seamless (and honestly clever) manner that impacts both your leadership and the business dynamics.

8

On Becoming the Leader Our World Needs Today

The final test of a leader is that he leaves behind him in other men, the conviction and the will to carry on.

—Walter Lippman

Humanity is evolving at a rapid pace, and this evolution is not physical but rather mental. Why the new world needs new leaders is not a hard statement to fathom. We see it in every direction, where juggernaut corporations deceive and distract us so that eyes are diverted from the real problem facing communities and environments impacted by their decisions. We are being tricked to look at the more subversive issues that usually revolve externally from the actual problem.

And the solution is quite simple. We spoke about it throughout this guide and by now you should be well acquainted with what it means. What the world needs is accountability!

I do not believe it to be some kind of naïve wish, but an actual solution! The technology and the media boom over the last 30 years have surely assisted in the plight of living in a more transparent world. Where groundbreaking discoveries are made and articles on lies and fraudulent behavior around politicians and executives are brought to light more frequently. Remember, it is doing the hard things that make more impact, and taking accountability for selfish and stupid choices is not easy.

Another very interesting aspect that has changed and might be here to stay is that of remote management. This is extensively apparent after the pandemic hit in 2020 where quarantine was tough, everything slowed down to a crawl, and many had no other choice but to start re-evaluating their life choices. When we have fewer distractions around us, we are able to observe where and how we use our time and energy. Some are quitting their office jobs to strive for a career that brings them more fulfillment at home. While many are acknowledging the impact of their daily consumerist lifestyle and the eventual impact stress has on their mental health.

Life carried on like normal until it didn't (if you get what I mean). The forced separation was never seriously preempted, and we had no real idea of what kinds of repercussions it would have on our mindsets and general work philosophy.

If anything, future leaders should be focusing on this more than ever! Sure, it is wonderful to be able to have meetings in your pajamas, but what impact will this have on the interpersonal aspects of leadership in the long term? Will the disengagement between employee and employer widen? Or will we be adapting to improve emotional awareness through remote communication devices?

The employee experience has diminished to measly percentages. The working from 'nine to five' model is being seriously rebranded and an attempt to supervise working hours is stepping up. Therefore, what I am saying is that leadership will have to evolve along with the environment that is being created. If it is more remote and screen-based, then it is imperative that a leader adapts to the medium and finds the right way to encourage, monitor, and challenge their followers at an equal pace.

Becoming the leader our world needs today means we need to start looking at those leadership styles, those development models, those communications skills that were discussed earlier and molding them to fit the space. It is a very exciting time for those who enjoy change!

The World Needs Leaders

We spend about 50% of our days in front of screens. It's a fact that the world is moving away from human interaction and towards remote communication.

How do our new emerging leaders change that around and become the glue that brings people together again? Already, we are aware of the gravity of the situation we find ourselves in, but we all too often feel like it is out of our control and that something bigger is at play. Yes, it's incredibly scary, but it is also incredibly intriguing.

If you are the leader we need today and for the next 50 years to come, then we need a challenger! A courageous and caring leader who does not look away from the problem but faces it with concern, clarity, and emotional maturity.

We can begin to connect with this theory by taking three aspects (which, by now, you should be familiar with) into account:

1. To become self-aware
2. To be aware of others
3. To know what is really important

The mindful and authentic leader of the world needs no title, no role, no financial backing. It's the integration of these three beacons of awareness that bring into the world people who can inspire others to be their best.

If you want to be a bigger part of tomorrow, then here are some of the noteworthy behaviors to adhere to:

- **Create your toolbox of leadership**
  Earlier, we touched upon the various leadership styles that you have, hopefully by now, discovered reflect your personal traits. But by expanding further and playing with all the different strengths in the various styles, then that proverbial toolbox gets bigger. The leader of tomorrow looks at the utensils before them and actively acknowledges when a tool is right for the job, and when it is not. The future leader is flexible and completely conscious of every choice's repercussions.

- **Care. Really care about them**
  We know now that being a true leader is not the position or the executive influence. You are a good leader because you genuinely care about others.

The job was never over when you got home and sat down for dinner. You know that while you were eating, you were still thinking of ways to make the environment in which you perform healthier and happier. How you care for your children, how you care for your parents, these feelings of unconditionality would apply to the job and followers to some degree as well.

- **Acknowledge the opinions of others**
  Yes, the opinion of the person on your team who is not always on the same viewpoint as your own. Rather than shying away from confronting them one to one, spend more time getting to know them so that you may better understand their input and reasoning. There is a dire need for a leader to hear them, resonate with their feelings, and come back with an outlook that incorporates theirs.

- **See in yourself the future**
  What I mean is be the person you know in your heart of hearts the world needs. I don't believe anyone is really too excited to watch the world burn. It's a saying of sociopaths, which any reasonable leader is surely not. Be ready to take the next step (which might be the hardest step you have ever taken) to be the best version of yourself. You will have to make some tough decisions with the power and knowledge available to you in that moment, so start by seeing that vision and making it a reality in small chunks, every day.

- **Get uncomfortable with not knowing**
  This begins with you getting out of your comfort zone. By embracing the chasms in your own

perception, you can start filling them with new information and fresh ideas. The world just does not stop for you, and by the time you think you should pull up your socks and make a choice, it might be too late. Not much else can grate the human spirit than the blemish of lost opportunities. Therefore, make sure you keep up to date with everything in your field of interest and always look outside of the box.

- **Become the chameleon of your life**
  Every surface you come into contact with influences you and your choices, especially in today's day and age. You are in constant flux with what is going on around you, always on the lookout for better ways to adjust in this fast-paced world. Rigidity can equal stagnation, and stagnation is eventual death. As I mentioned, we do not just talk about business strategies. We talk about the people who live within these strategies. Whatever is scary and new should be seen as something mighty fun to learn and develop.

What can be judged as a detrimental factor in building the leaders of tomorrow is the education model many countries still use today in early to middle childhood. The system that has been around for centuries is falling short of the honest needs of the leader and followers that are to come. If a more integral and modern curriculum was implemented through social skills, financial intelligence, and mental health, then we could potentially see a future where the employee and employer relationship is stable and optimistic.

If a greater value was set on human needs and growing individual talents to benefit the whole team, then we could begin to see a future with less subdivision and disregard for others.

Behind the Scenes of Great Leadership

We often see the boss as an island of knowledge and responsibility. Something foreign that you think you might never be able to understand. A man or woman standing at the top of that cold mountain just maintaining the larger idea of the company or team. It can make it hard to approach them with "trivial" issues that you fear will bring a dismissal or disregard.

The truth is that great leaders are as humble in their own pursuit of knowledge as you are. They do not know everything, but they know some things with mastery.

What have we evaluated so far with regards to good leadership? Leaders...

- ...are kind but with a firm hand.
- ...earned their trust honorably.
- ...are sentimental and pragmatic.
- ...understand their ego well.
- ...initiate change because they have an eye for potential.
- ...actions and words are always compatible.
- ...control is wide, but not stringent.

Great leadership is always at work, even when the curtain closes because a good portion of leadership does indeed happen backstage.

What do these leaders do that accelerates their success in both their followers and their individual capacities? Well, these leaders are:

1. **Fighting for others.** They are putting their neck on the line for the opportunity to show and not tell. They are reacting proactively to problems, facing them head-on, and showing their followers that they can do the same if they lean into their fear of the unknown and have faith in themselves.

2. **Focusing on course correction, not course obstruction.** The mentorship role of these leaders is their ability to hold the follower's hand and show them the right way to go. Great leaders stand up for them, believe in them, and show them their own path to success.

3. **Making inclusivity imperative.** The leader does not win, the team wins. Imagine if only the captain of the FIFA winning team was standing on that stage lifting the trophy above their heads. That would be preposterous! The entire team celebrates together. This is what leadership does, it acknowledges the hard work of bringing people together to be great, and when the win is received, it includes everyone.

4. **Using their power to empower.** You fight for them, you guide them, you include them. Now it is time to understand how to give them that strength to do the same for the next person.

When a leader understands that the more intimate reasonings of leadership happen backstage, then the impact of their beliefs becomes greater than the impact of their image.

The great leaders of our now and tomorrow will not brand themselves, they will not run away from consequences and hide behind expensive lawyers when things go pear-shaped. They are authentic and integral to the team as the team is to them. When a leader can honestly say that profits come secondary to people, then they are on the right track.

Image is not reality, and we need a real flesh and blood human being to guide us forward. Recognizing that to breed and nurture humans with the courage to face the music when they deviate from the set path is in itself acceptance and accountability. Exploration and innovation have been our motto for most of our time on this planet. So, let us now evolve our mindsets to inclusion, integrity, and respect.

Create Your Leadership Development Plan

The leadership development plan has one purpose: to grow you as a leader. This is taking the time to sit down with yourself and personally look at what you are and what you could be.

Sometimes in the more inclusive work environments, we can see employers making these development plans available to their employees, by including them into the employees' contracts, galvanizing their belief in the mission. Their leadership plan is stipulated for everyone to see, and this brings honesty to the field.

Like anything in life, a plan starts with a good look in the mirror. The leader assesses their own mental health, their own reasons for wanting to implement these plans, and all the short to long-term goals that come with it. Once that is ironed out, then a developmental plan can be built around the core reasons.

The elements that breathe life into your plan are:

1. **Aligning your skills with your goals**
   You have big plans, big dreams, therefore your skill set should be running to keep up and learn as much as possible, so you may be well prepared when that door of opportunity opens. I have spoken about being proactive, but it needs to be drilled into your mind for you to really appreciate its power.

   Find out what are the core skills that you have to harness with care and work on them. This is done by both shadowing others who already possess this quality so as to learn from them, as well as approaching external methods of learning.

2. **Finding the vacuum**
   Not the vacuum cleaner, but finding the vacuum where nothing seems to happen and turning it around, making it new, and successfully solving it. The new leader needs to be putting themselves in the path of gaining skill sets that challenge these vacuums and elevate their expertise in seeing solutions everywhere.

   By taking on projects that are slightly out of your normal range of responsibilities, you can prove yourself to those that look out for your improvement. In critical situations when decisions need to be made with precision, stretch your capacities for solving, including, and leading the group.

3. **Growing relationships**
   Here, you need to determine who in your environment has the need and interest in building a connection with you. This, in its entirety, should be a general aspect of the leader, but when the individual leader can recognize where they can learn, teach, and build skills in a mutually beneficial way, then a strong relationship should be attained.

   This is not schmoozing. It is relating to someone who resonates with your own needs and who is willing to be a part of the symbiotic relationship

4. **Designating tasks strategically**
   We have discussed this in previous chapters, but of course, this little observation is vital. The wisdom and experience required to juggle your time and that of your followers are of the utmost importance. People are looking up to you to make things happen, so you cannot afford to wait for them to be ready. You need to push them to perform and grow and see their own potential.

   That is where you step in and carefully evaluate where you can start passing on more complex tasks to more competent followers while focusing on your own individual jobs. The balance is key!

5. **Calendarizing your actions**
   The greatest minds of our time did not use to-do lists, they calendarized actions that needed to be done. By stipulating what the task is, what time of the day it needs to be done, and how long the task will take, they have already in their minds performed it. It is already completed because all

the small variables have been actioned onto that calendar the day before.

It is a whole lot easier to start your day with a very scheduled mental space that brings step-by-step actions to be performed. You are essentially micromanaging yourself, but it is a fantastic tool to increase performance.

6. **Evaluating overall success indicators**

And the most important factor throughout this whole list is, in fact, never keeping your eye off the ball. I have asked you to learn to look at followers as an extension of yourself. You treat them like you wish to be treated. But it is undeniably important that you also always keep an eye on the performance levels of the team as a whole. Success indicators are the quality of work, preparation and strategic planning, team morale, and responsibility delegation, to name a few.

The leader has one eye on the team and one eye on the prize. Without forgetting the mission statement, they are always able to help and guide those who have.

Please note that your personal development plan is, first and foremost, malleable. I cannot stress this further, leadership means really knowing how to rearrange and rediagnose the processes that might have become easy and monotonous. You will always be building new skills, new outlooks on work and life, and new relationships that influence you along the way. So this development plan will never have the opportunity to get dusty, as it will need reform on a regular basis while still adhering to your core values.

When creating this plan and translating it into a graph or diagram for easy visual representation, it is important that it be neat, coordinated, and include all the variables and principles that keep the plan in a circulatory learning system. The variables to incorporate are always feedback, mentorship, self-reflection, and proactive learning.

Remember, you can passively read this book and really not be finding the point of the whole matter. But by kneading at the aspects I have given to you about the whole concept and philosophy, you will be able to grasp the gravity of your role and what impacts you can actually make on others.

Words of Wisdom From the World's Greatest Leaders

I am sure that you will be aware of some of the quotes that I have resourced below, but maybe what you are not aware of is their deeper and more intricate meaning. The beauty of famous sayings from human beings that have lived in the past and achieved incredible success is that they break down the basics of leadership in a single sentence thanks to the sheer time spent within it.

It is elevated to a grandness, almost an unachievable goal of leadership that sometimes makes people shy away from its grandeur. I want you to read each of these quotes out loud. When the thing is said, it becomes more powerful.

A leader is best when people barely know he exists. When his work is done, his aim fulfilled, they will say: we did it ourselves.

—Lao Tzu

Lao Tzu wrote *The Art of War* and was an incredible leader with critical thinking attributes that many use today for the basis of their own strategies and successes in achieving something. The message is simple, don't show your input, show your resolve and let the success be theirs.

When you can't make them see the light, make them feel the heat.

—Ronald Reagan

Known as one of the most popular presidents in American history, Reagan was very optimistic about his views. But as emphasized by his quote, sometimes a line must be drawn when things need to be done and finalized and remembering your role of keeping it all together in a patient but stern manner.

Don't find fault, find a remedy.

—Henry Ford

It is certainly true that the more people surround you, the more things have the tendency to get tense at some point. Therefore, when dealing with mistakes, new employee errors, or changes in the plan, it is valuable to learn not to rush into picking at the omission but rather waste no time in seeing how it can be turned around. A positive outlook changes everything!

Outstanding leaders go out of their way to boost the self-esteem of their personnel. If people believe in themselves, it's amazing what they can accomplish.

—Sam Walton

This one is pretty straightforward, right? Walton founded Walmart, and that is a business that prides itself on its people. Therefore, by giving them the space (keyword here) to make their own impact and be recognized as an integral member of the team, then that elevates their interest in their job and in the company's goal.

There is no other way to guard yourself against flattery than by making men understand that telling the truth will not offend you.

—Niccoló Machiavelli

This one is particularly eye-opening, as you would expect from the 14th-century Italian diplomat known for his knifing characteristics. But this quote is as true as it gets. Stay on the straight line of truth, be boldly honest with your followers, and show that loyalty requires no false pretenses.

Leadership is a privilege to better the lives of others. It is not an opportunity to satisfy personal greed.

—Mwai Kibaki

The Kenyan politician spoke these words, even though some may argue that he didn't listen to his own advice. Look, the obvious human sin of natural greed in human psychology has affected us all at one time in our lives. But as we get older and begin stepping into the shoes of true leadership, the principle will always be about putting this sin last! (Or throwing it away completely, if possible).

Every morning I look in the mirror and say, "I could have done three things better yesterday."

—Jeff Immelt

Once the poster child of business innovation, Immelt was CEO of General Electric for almost 17 years, and you can imagine the time and passion given in that position of authority. We can see that when you are consumed by the innovative bug and you are in the groove of things, then you become more aware of what you can actively do every day to innovate and be better for them.

The test of leadership is not to put greatness into humanity, but to elicit it, for the greatness is already there.

—James Buchanan

It is the true test indeed! If you can handle knowing that your only role in this beautiful game is to allow others to find their personal best, then that's brilliant! No matter where they go, or what they eventually become, you saw something in their eyes, a passion for life and learning. Find those people and show them how to be great.

If you command wisely, you will be obeyed cheerfully.
—Thomas Fuller

The English historian certainly wasn't incorrect with this authoritarian quote. The question of how you run your ship will depend on how you run your crew. You may command, but then you better know exactly what you are doing, so that orders are obeyed constantly and mistakes become rare. The point here is that the more you know your job, the more confident and calm you appear to your team. Show pride and confidence in your choices.

What you may notice about these quotes is that maybe one would not be considered a great leader, at least not now, looking back. And yes, some viewpoints are drastically different, some statements may be argued to be totally incorrect, but one thing stood true: they were acutely aware of their people's needs.

They knew what kind of leader they were, and they understood the audience and how they could bring their followers together to stand for something and be strong in their unity. Yes, some agendas were pushed, profits were made, limits were tested, and these leaders at some point lost the plot and went rogue. But the human errors we make are not set in stone. A great leader recognizes where they have disappointed their followers, and learns how to move forward so it never happens again under their watch.

Conclusion

Do what you feel in your heart to be right, for you will be criticized anyway.

—Eleanor Roosevelt

I wanted to end this book on a high note that incorporates factful observation and a tender truth, which is summarized in the above quote by the former First Lady of the US. It is impossible to be liked by all, but it is very possible to still walk the path with a clear conscience and an honest dream.

You will be talked about whether you do good or bad in this world. The question is, will you be the one to step up to the podium and voice your intentions with conviction and truth?

If you feel a certain way about something and if you truly find that what you have in mind will not hurt anyone, but possibly set something straight, then do it! Do not sit there every day wondering what people may think, but rather say to yourself that the heart within you is never wrong. It tells you when something is right and when something is off balance. If you follow that primal guide to survival, then whatever choice you make, whether it succeeds or fails, will bring you to a closer version of total truth.

I hope that by now you have felt that relationship of understanding and motivation (you, the reader, and I, the mentor) towards being the complete leader your followers, or future followers, will need.

Some of my peers feel unconsciously irritated when I say that the most powerful thing in the world is love, often responding with, "Oh, don't be so silly, Paul!" But I stand true to this statement day in and day out. Our hearts beat within our chests, and we feel more of a connection to something when our pulse rate increases, when the blood starts rushing to our face, and when the energy and excitement bubble to the surface. These emotions are natural and above all, needed. We no longer care for the statuesque leader that watches but never cares. We need more! Much, much more!

I am so proud of you for getting this far and accepting the challenge to step up, make that choice to care, and believe in people who care and believe in you. Your vision of a future that brings more acceptance, more aligned productivity, and tons of enjoyment is what the world is desperately calling out for.

So, you have read this book, tested your own character, and set goals for yourself to improve and evolve each day. I must ask, what does meaningful leadership mean to you now? Take a moment to clarify the concepts you have learned so as to justify the actions that you will make. Something must have changed, clicked, shifted within to allow you to visualize a wider spectrum.

If you can do me one favor before you close this book, please recognize the tunnel vision syndrome and promise me that you will always have an open heart and mind so that the world does not pass you by. Be free, be open, be conscious of all things that you come into contact with.

Assess how they resonate with you and decide to either take them or leave them! That is it.

You have established which leadership style fits you and why you fit it so well. You have most likely seen which leadership styles you could never respect, helping you see what you should never become. By learning what leadership really is, you can now judge other leaders around you with a keener eye (which is always advised). You know the qualities, the traits, and the roles that it encompasses, so focus on them with all your might.

The methods and models to develop your skills and systems of leadership have been revealed to you. The addition of an interest in finding better ways to lead has encouraged you to always evolve and focus your attention on being the leader that believes in their own capabilities and those of the team that works by your side.

The next time you have to communicate with meaning and intent, you know how to approach each situation with tact and skill. I think I have drilled that into you quite a bit already, even though it is never enough. I have given you an idea of how your words, your tone, and your body language all play a huge role in bringing people to appeal to your character, enjoy what you say, and commit to your vision and moral code.

Along with communication, we saw interpersonal skills and the expertise development to decision making and solving small to large problems that happen on a daily basis with tact and structure.

"If we are to build tomorrow's leaders today, we need to anticipate what skills, temperaments, and specific competencies will be valued as we face future needs. If the past is a predictor of the future, the world of tomorrow will be characterized by rapid change, new technology, greater diversity, increased globalization, and the need for lifelong learning" (Genovese, 2014).

Finally, as stated in the above quote, the world is changing so fast that the new leaders emerging into the scene need to already be sprinting when they jump in. While at the same time, it's asking older generations of leaders to adapt, innovate, and bring about change in their own way too.

You are the future of this planet, and by now, we know that this planet needs better humans to make better decisions. We need this to inspire future generations in their own unique quests to improve society and its preconceptions. Go out there and find what makes you tick. If you have a passion to be a role model for years to come, then forge your own path but never forget the mission statement.

And for the last time, thank you! You are already initiating change by asking how you can increase your knowledge and pass it onto the next phase of leaders to come. Have fun being who you are and always do it with love, compassion, and pride!

References

Avolio, B. J. (2005). *Leadership Development in Balance.* Lawrence Erlbaum.

Baker, A. (2016). *Simplicity (Stanford Encyclopedia of Philosophy).* Stanford.Edu. https://plato.stanford. edu/entries/simplicity/

Ball, P. (2016). *The Tyranny of Simple Explanations.* The Atlantic. https://www.theatlantic.com/science/ archive/2016/08/occams-razor/495332/

Becker, B. (2020). *The 8 Most Common Leadership Styles & How to Find Your Own [Quiz].* Hubspot. https:// blog.hubspot.com/marketing/leadership-styles

Bowen, J. (2017). *Why your interpersonal skills will define you as a leader.* Ambition Institute. https://www. ambition.org.uk/blog/how-interpersonal-skills-define-you-as-a-leader/

British Heart Foundation. (2018). *10 tips for active listening.* https://www.bhf.org.uk/ informationsupport/heart-matters-magazine/ wellbeing/how-to-talk-about-health-problems/active-listening

Brown, B. (2018). *Dare to Lead: Brave Work. Tough Conversations. Whole Hearts.* Random House.

Capture Your Flag. (2012). *Simon Sinek on What It Means to Be a Leader* [Video]. YouTube. https://www. youtube.com/watch?v=VwbkzODSkHU

Caredda, S. (2021). *Leadership Models: The Theory and the Practice*. Sergio Caredda. https://sergiocaredda.eu/ organisation/leadership-models-the-theory-and-the-practice/

Changeboard team. (2019). *Problem solving vs decision making – what is the difference?* Changeboard. https:// www.changeboard.com/article-details/16960/ problem-solving-vs-decision-making-what-is-the-difference-/

Cherry, K. (2020). *5 Ways to Become More Emotionally Intelligent at Work*. Verywell Mind. https://www. verywellmind.com/utilizing-emotional-intelligence-in-the-workplace-4164713

Cherry, K. (2020). *What Are Prominent Leadership Styles and Frameworks You Should Know?* Verywell Mind. https://www.verywellmind.com/leadership-styles-2795312

Clarinval, P. (2021). *Want To Be A Great Leader? The First Step Is Self-Awareness.* Forbes. https://www.forbes.com/sites/ forbeshumanresourcescouncil/2021/07/26/ want-to-be-a-great-leader-the-first-step-is-self-awareness/?sh=16d30d1d6bf7

Clear, J. (2017). *First Principles: Elon Musk on the Power of Thinking for Yourself.* James Clear. https://jamesclear. com/first-principles

Collins, J. (2001). *Good to Great: Why Some Companies Make the Leap and Others Don't.* HarperBusiness.

Collins, J. (2014). *Jim Collins - Concepts - The Hedgehog Concept.* Jim Collins. https://www.jimcollins.com/concepts/the-hedgehog-concept.html

Connolly, M. (2018). *7 Strong Leadership Scenarios: How Do You Measure Up?* Neways Somatic Psychotherapy & Coaching. https://newayscenter.com/7-strong-leadership-scenarios/

Crisp Studio. (2020). *4 mental models for a better decision making process.* https://www.crisp.studio/blog/mental-models-decision-making-process

Dunne, C. (2019). *40 Team Communication Quotes to Inspire Your Team.* Tameday. https://www.tameday.com/team-communication-quotes/

Evans, E. (2016). *106 Quotes on How to Be an Effective and Inspiring Leader.* Bright Drops. https://brightdrops.com/leadership-quotes

Genovese, M. A. (2013). *Building Tomorrow's Leaders Today: On Becoming a Polymath Leader.* Routledge.

George Mason University. (2019). *Core Leadership Values.* https://masonleads.gmu.edu/about-us/core-leadership-values/

Goldfish Consulting. (2017). *What is Personal, Interpersonal and Professional Leadership?* https://goldfish-consulting.co.za/services/what-personal-interpersonal-and-professional-leadership

Hicham Fleihan. (2021). *Warren Buffett and Charlie Munger A Wealth of Wisdom* [Video]. Vimeo. https://vimeo.com/569939634

Juneja, P. (2019). *Importance of Leadership.* Managementstudyguide.Com. https://www.managementstudyguide.com/importance_of_leadership.htm

Kohntopp, T., & Mccann, J. (2019). *Virtual Leadership in Organizations: Potential Competitive Virtual Leadership in Organizations: Potential Competitive Advantage?* Walden University. https://scholarworks.waldenu.edu/cgi/viewcontent.cgi?article=1148&context=sm_pubs

Kruse, K. (2012). *100 Best Quotes On Leadership.* Forbes. https://www.forbes.com/sites/kevinkruse/2012/10/16/quotes-on-leadership/?sh=601cb61b2feb

Kumar, A. (2021). *First Principles Thinking Explained with Examples.* Data Analytics. https://vitalflux.com/first-principles-thinking-explained-with-examples/

LearningREADefined. (2016). *How To Be A Leader - The 7 Great Leadership Traits* [Video]. YouTube. https://www.youtube.com/watch?v=2lEp4TVpxgA

Lewis, R. (2020). *What the World Needs Now Is Great Leadership.* The Robin Report. https://www.therobinreport.com/what-the-world-needs-now-is-great-leadership/

Lumen. (2010). *Developing Leadership Skills | Boundless Management*. https://courses.lumenlearning.com/ boundless-management/chapter/developing-leadership-skills/

Luthra, A., & Richa Dahiya, D. (2015). *Effective leadership is all about communicating effectively: Connecting leadership and communication 1*. International Journal of Management and Business Studies. https://www. mcgill.ca/engage/files/engage/effective_leadership_ is_all_about_communicating_effectively_luthra_ dahiya_2015.pdf

Manson, M. (2021). *Mark Manson* [Video]. YouTube. https://www.youtube.com/channel/ UCOTnW9acNxqeojxXDMbohcA

Marquet, D. (2012). *Turn the Ship Around!: How to Create Leadership at Every Level*. Greenleaf Book Group Press.

Marr, B. (2021). *The Most Motivational Leadership Quotes*. Bernard Marr. https://bernardmarr.com/the-most-motivational-leadership-quotes/

Martinuzzi, B. (2019). *Leadership Styles and How to Find Your Own*. American Express. https://www. americanexpress.com/en-us/business/trends-and-insights/articles/the-7-most-common-leadership-styles-and-how-to-find-your-own/

Matthews, D. (2021). *How to Solve Problems Successfully Using the Power of Inversion*. The Resolve Blog. https://www.resolve.blog/articles/inversion

Mazza, S. (2020). *What Is The Best Definiton of Leadership?* Random Acts Of Leadership. https://randomactsofleadership.com/best-definition-of-leadership/

McClung, J. (2017). *Simon Sinek - Understanding Empathy* [Video]. YouTube. https://www.youtube.com/watch?v=pi86Nr9Mdms&t=216s

Moore, C. (2019). *15 Communication Exercises and Games for the Workplace.* PositivePsychology.Com. https://positivepsychology.com/communication-exercises-for-work/

Morgan, J. (2020). *What is leadership, and who is a leader?* Chief Learning Officer - CLO Media. https://www.chieflearningofficer.com/2020/01/06/what-is-leadership-and-who-is-a-leader/

Muse, T. (2019). *Are leaders born or made?* HRD. https://www.hrdconnect.com/are-leaders-born-or-made/

Myatt, M. (2014). *10 Communication Secrets Of Great Leaders.* Forbes. https://www.forbes.com/sites/mikemyatt/2012/04/04/10-communication-secrets-of-great-leaders/?sh=1834967122fe

Myers, C. (2016). *How I Learned That Employees Need A Leader, Not A Friend.* Forbes. https://www.forbes.com/sites/chrismyers/2016/09/08/how-i-learned-that-employees-need-a-leader-not-a-friend/?sh=789a8a434d45

Nonaka, I., & Takeuchi, H. (2016). *The Big Idea: The Wise Leader*. Harvard Business Review. https://hbr.org/2011/05/the-big-idea-the-wise-leader

O'Keefe, P. (2018). *The Strengths & Weaknesses of Today's Emerging Leaders*. Edge Training Systems. https://www.edgetrainingsystems.com/the-strengths-weaknesses-of-todays-emerging-leaders/

Psychology Compass. (2019). *Identifying and successfully implementing your leadership style*. https://psychologycompass.com/blog/leadership-style/

R. (2021). *What is a Thought Leader?* Thought Leadership Lab. https://thoughtleadershiplab.com/what-is-a-thought-leader/

Risi, J. (2016). *Why the Best Leaders Actually Work Behind the Scene*. Fortune. https://fortune.com/2016/10/10/how-to-be-a-great-leader-advice/

Robbins, T. (2019). *7 Ways of Developing Leadership Skills | Improve Your Leadership Skills*. Tonyrobbins.Com. https://www.tonyrobbins.com/leadership-impact/7-ways-to-improve-leadership-skills/

Rooke, D., & Torbert, W. R. (2005). *Seven Transformations of Leadership*. Harvard Business Review.

Sauers, D., Marchesseault, K., Mandel, M., Michaels, M., Chertudi, M., Brodersen, C., Boyer, C., & Hills, C. (2016). *The Secret Handshake: Effective Communication Strategies for the Workplace*. Kendall Hunt Publishing.

Schyns, B., & Hansbrough, T. (2010). *When Leadership Goes Wrong: Destructive Leadership, Mistakes, and Ethical Failures.* Information Age Publishing.

Simon Lancaster. (2016). *Speak like a leader | Simon Lancaster | TEDxVerona* [Video]. YouTube. https://www.youtube.com/watch?v=bGBamfWasNQ&t=320s

SlideModel. (2021). *Six Leadership Styles Relationship vs Task Curve for PowerPoint.* https://slidemodel.com/templates/six-leadership-styles-relationship-vs-task-curve-for-powerpoint/

Soundview Executive Book Summaries. (2019). *The 25 Best Leadership Books of All-Time.* Soundview Magazine. https://www.summary.com/magazine/the-25-best-leadership-books-of-all-time/

Stark, P. B. (2017). *Are You the Leader the World Needs You to Be?* Peter Barron Stark Companies. https://peterstark.com/leader-world-needs/

Success Magazine. (2014). *Leaders, Learn the Right Way to Make Mistakes* [Video]. YouTube. https://www.youtube.com/watch?v=gQPSvbDTe8M

TEDX Talks. (2016). *Great leadership comes down to only two rules | Peter Anderton | TEDxDerby* [Video]. YouTube. https://www.youtube.com/watch?v=oDsMlmfLjd4&t=238s

The Michael Page Team. (2020). *How interpersonal skills affect your leadership style.* Michael Page. https://www.michaelpage.com.au/advice/

management-advice/leadership/how-interpersonal-skills-affect-your-leadership-style

The National Society of Leadership and Success. (2017). *Leaders are Made, Not Born––Starting in School.* https://nslsfacts.org/2017/07/28/leaders-are-made-not-born-starting-in-school/

Thomas, A. (2017). *15 Traits of the Worst Leaders (Avoid at All Costs).* Inc.Com. https://www.inc.com/andrew-thomas/15-traits-of-the-worst-leaders-avoid-at-all-costs.html

Thompson, M. (2020). *4 Ways to Get Your Communication Tight without Saying A Word.* SIMPLE. https://medium.com/simple-pub/how-to-sharpen-your-communication-skills-without-saying-a-word-5de5b4717899

Todorovic, J. (2020). *7 Techniques for Effective Leadership Negotiation Process.* RLX Business Solutions. https://relax.ph/blog/leadership-negotiation/

Tomasko, R. M. (2002). *Seven Models of Leadership Development.* Www.Roberttomasko.Com. http://www.roberttomasko.com/Consult.7ModelsLead.html

Tracy, B. (2017). *5 Different Types of Leadership Styles | Brian Tracy* [Video]. YouTube. https://www.youtube.com/watch?v=vilZazhIjoc

TWOWP. (2019). *The Seven Transformations of Leadership: A Simple Summary.* The World of Work Project. https://worldofwork.io/2019/07/the-7-transformations-of-leadership/

USI Web Services. (2018). *Five roles of a leader - University of Southern Indiana.* Usi.Edu. https://www.usi.edu/outreach/engage/2017-archives/five-roles-of-a-leader/

Walia, C. (2020). *Role of A Leader* [Video]. YouTube. https://www.youtube.com/watch?v=4zzClpfRln8

Williams, R. L., & Cothrel, J. P. (1997). Building tomorrow's leaders today. *Strategy & Leadership, 25*(5), 17–22. https://doi.org/10.1108/eb054596

Women and Leadership Australia. (2017). *Do you have these 4 leadership weaknesses?* Wla.Edu.Au. https://www.wla.edu.au/do-you-have-these.html

Printed in Great Britain
by Amazon

17877710R00088